Shipwrecks, Scalawags, and Scavengers

The Storied Waters of Pigeon Point

To Harry —
Wishing you safe passage.
J Aven S.

SHIPWRECKS, SCALAWAGS, AND SCAVENGERS

THE STORIED WATERS OF PIGEON POINT

BY

JOANN SEMONES

THE GLENCANNON PRESS

MARITIME BOOKS

Palo Alto
2007

Published by The Glencannon Press
P.O. Box 341, Palo Alto, CA 94302
Tel. 800-711-8985, Fax. 510-528-3194
www.glencannon.com

The photograph on the cover is courtesy of Rudy and Alice Rico (www.rudyalicelighthouse.net). The illustration used on the endpapers is courtesy of the San Francisco Maritime National Historical Park.

First Edition, first printing.

Library of Congress Cataloging-in-Publication Data

Semones, JoAnn, 1945-
  Shipwrecks, scalawags and scaventers : the storied waters of Pigeon Point / by JoAnn Semones.
      p. cm.
  Includes bibliographical references and index.
  ISBN 978-1-889901-42-8 (alk. paper)
  1. Shipwrecks--California--Pigeon Point (San Mateo County) -- History.
  2. Pigeon Point (San Mateo County, Calif.)--History, Naval. I. Title

F868.S19S46 2007
910.9164'32--dc22
                                    2007030668

Publisher's note: Every effort is made to obtain and reproduce the best quality photographs. Due to the age of the photos available, some are of a lesser quality. They have nevertheless been used.

DEDICATION

For Julie Barrow,
who taught me to
"stay in the boat."

ACKNOWLEDGEMENTS

Writing a book is both a solitary and a collaborative effort. It's not unlike being on a ship at sea. Each person has a specific responsibility, yet also relies on other crew members to keep the vessel sailing in the right direction. And so it has been in bringing this volume to a safe harbor.

The voyage began eight years ago, when I became a docent at Pigeon Point Lighthouse. Learning about the tower's history, tramping around the grounds in fair weather and foul, and sharing the companionship of dedicated volunteers lit a spark that continues to burn today. My special thanks to Nelson Morosini and Judy Pfeil. You trained me well.

Later, I found further inspiration during discussions with members of the National Marine Sanctuary Program involving the development of an interpretive center at Pigeon Point. In preparing the text for the exhibit, I uncovered far more information than could be used. This was especially true regarding the shipwrecks, so colleagues urged me to write a book. My heartfelt appreciation goes to Dawn Hayes and Carol Preston. You gave me the idea.

Researching the book meant many hours spent in archives, libraries, and maritime museums. Invaluable assistance was provided by Cathy Williamson and Claudia Jew of The Mariners' Museum in Newport News, Virginia; Carol Peterson of the San Mateo County History Museum; John Hedger and Bob Glass of the National Archives and Records Administration in San Bruno; Tim Thomas of the Maritime Museum of Monterey; and Steve Davenport of the J. Porter Shaw Library at the San Francisco Maritime National Historical Park. You are all diligent and patient beyond belief.

Writing the book meant more hours creating each ship's story. I am indebted to my creative comrade, Shannon Nottestad, and to my sister, Vicky Semones, who pored over drafts and revisions. You encouraged me to follow my instincts and my heart.

Finally, eternal gratitude goes to my partner, Julie Barrow, for supporting my "maritime madness." Without you, I could not have completed the voyage.

— J.A.S.

CONTENTS

ILLUSTRATIONS

PROLOGUE

Between 1853 and 1953, ships of all types — clipper ships, barks, schooners, and steamers — sailing the central California coast fell victim to Pigeon Point's unpredictable weather and rocky shoreline.

Mariners knew the hazards well. Thick haze lingered persistently, obscuring familiar landmarks and concealing ships at sea. Engulfed in the dense "pea soup" fog common along these shores, navigational readings were often unreliable. Even signals from fog horns and other vessels could be easily misinterpreted.

Further forces of nature awaited. Unruly currents, brutal waves, and tempestuous winds stirred Pigeon Point's deep, moody waters. Jagged reefs beneath the surface and monumental rocks protruding above snagged many a hapless vessel.

Several of the wrecks occurred between Pigeon Point and Año Nuevo Point, also known as New Year's Point. The two sites are in such close proximity — just five miles apart — that their locations were often recorded interchangeably. For that reason, shipwrecks attributed to either area are included in this book.

Although most disasters occurred under similar conditions, each shipwreck tells its own unique story. Sailors and salvagers, hard work and bad luck, business schemes and personal dreams all appear. Yet, each represents more than colorful sea lore.

Each shipwreck is an important portal to our past, a significant part of our maritime heritage, linking us to unforgettable times, noteworthy places, and remarkable people.

If it is true that every ship has her own soul, then every shipwreck has a spirit waiting to be rediscovered. It is a voyage worth taking.

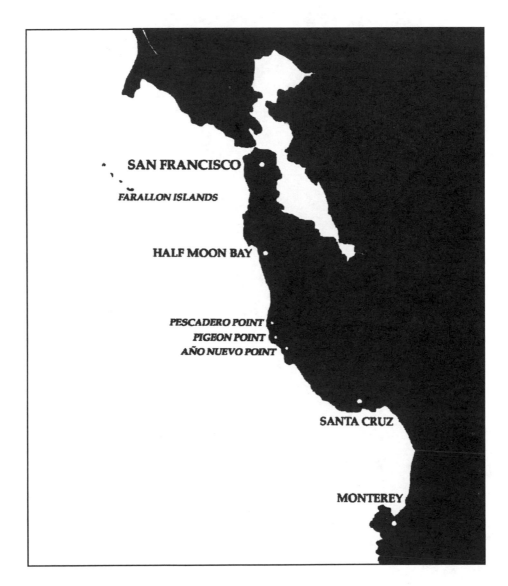

The central coast of California.
Courtesy of Janet Taggart.

INTRODUCTION

Located fifty miles south of San Francisco, Pigeon Point's diverse and abundant natural resources have drawn people to the area for centuries. The earliest inhabitants, called Quiroste, lived there over 11,000 years ago. Today, these Native Californians are known as the Ohlone.

Marine life was plentiful and gray whales were a common sight. In the 1600s, Spanish mariners began charting the area. They named it *"Punta de las Balenas"* or Whale Point. In the 1820s, Portuguese whalers from the Azores turned the cove into a whaling station and small shipping center.

The nearby community of Pescadero, which means "fishing place" in Spanish, was established to take advantage of a vast natural supply of trout, and later supported prosperous farms, dairies, and orchards. The region exported whale oil, tallow, potatoes, butter, cheese, beans, grain, lumber, and hides.

In 1848, the Gold Rush dramatically increased the number of ships sailing along California's coast. Far more emigrants came by sea than overland, and vessels of all types carried gold-seekers and goods to the booming town of San Francisco. The Pacific Coast, commonly called the "Maritime West," flourished with maritime industries.

However, prosperity came fraught with problems. Huge cargoes of food, supplies, and passengers perished in shipwrecks. In 1853, one wreck was so memorable that Whale Point was renamed Pigeon Point for the clipper ship that sank there.

In 1871, after many shipwrecks, the loss of many lives, and much public outcry, a fog signal was placed at Pigeon Point. In 1872, another fog signal went into service at Año Nuevo Point (just south of Pigeon

Point) and a lighthouse was built at Pigeon Point. Eventually, fifty-nine lighthouses were constructed along California's shores.

Unfortunately, even the lighthouse could not prevent shipwrecks. Over the years, unpredictable weather and human error led to other maritime tragedies. What follows is the history of those events.

1

An Enduring Legacy

June 6, 1853

S he made only a single voyage, yet she left an enduring legacy. The *Carrier Pigeon* is remembered as one of the finest clipper ships of her day. The point where she foundered is a lasting tribute to her memory and to an era we will never see again.

The Age of Sail

The 1840s to 1860s are often referred to as the Golden Age of Sail. The era began in 1843 as a result of the growing demand for more rapid delivery of tea from China to England, continued under the provocative influence of the discovery of gold in California in 1848 and Australia in 1851, and ended in 1869 when the U.S. transcontinental railroad was completed. Linking the eastern United States with California on the Pacific Coast, the railway network revolutionized America's transportation system.

During the Age of Sail, magnificent clipper ships, such as the *Carrier Pigeon*, dotted the seas. "Clipper," an American term for a fast sailing vessel, was first applied to speedy schooners and brigs developed at Baltimore for use as privateers, pilot boats, and fast transports. It was

Boston Harbor as it appeared in 1853 with clipper ships like the Carrier Pigeon *arriving and departing.* The Mariners' Museum.

said that clippers went after the wind, rather than waiting for the wind to come to them.

These "greyhounds of the sea" delivered mail, passengers, and manufactured goods at record speeds between the East and West coasts. From the beginning of the great California gold rush to the opening of cross-country rail service, nearly all commerce between the Pacific and Atlantic oceans was conducted by these swift ships.

Best Modeled Clipper Ship

When the *Carrier Pigeon* sailed from Boston in 1853, she was hailed by local newspapers as "the best modeled clipper ship that has gone out of Kennebec this season, built and finished in the best manner." Launched at Bath, Maine in 1852 by Trufant, Drummond & Company, the sleek, square-rigged vessel had a knife-like bow, narrow mid-body, and deep, straight keel. She was 175 feet long, with a beam of 34 feet, and measured 843 tons.

She boasted a hand-carved gilded figurehead of a pigeon in flight fixed just beneath her bowsprit. Symbolizing the legendary and hallowed history of the message-bearing carrier pigeon, the golden winged bird was meant to inspire the crew. The carrier pigeon was an omen of good luck — fast, dependable, ever returning.

The *Carrier Pigeon*, carrying 1,300 tons of general merchandise, was 130 days out of Boston when she was thrown off course. Having rounded Cape Horn at the tip of South America, she had traveled more than 15,000 miles. The trip around "Cape Stiff," as sailors called it, was not an easy one. "Sudden squalls of winds and fog called willewaks dash with violence over the high lands," one mariner observed, "and in a few minutes shut the scene from view."

Cape Horn's mountainous waves and 100-mile-an-hour gales tested the stamina of even the hardiest ship and crew. Yet, challenges along Pacific shores were equally fierce. With its rocky out-croppings, heavy surf, strong currents, and thick fog banks, California's coast was one of the most notoriously treacherous in the world. Even knowing this, the crew of the *Carrier Pigeon* could not have foreseen her fate.

Wreck Ashore

On June 6, 1853, lost in heavy fog and besieged by strong northwest winds, the *Carrier Pigeon* was dangerously off course. The wandering clipper came to grief on a craggy out-cropping of rocks not far from San Francisco, her intended destination. Fifteen minutes after the vessel struck, seven feet of water were in the hold. In half an hour, water was above the lower deck.

"Her bow lay about 500 feet from the beach," reports said, "and she rests amidships on a ledge of rocks which have broken the ship's back. The tide ebbs and flows in her." The *Carrier Pigeon's* maiden voyage from Boston to San Francisco had ended in calamity. Mercifully, the crew was rescued, but the hapless vessel became the focus of contentious salvage disputes and further disaster.

To settlers in the isolated coastal village of Pescadero, a three-masted sailing vessel stranded just yards from shore was a novel sight. It was also a unique opportunity to appropriate ship's booty. Crying "Wreck Ashore!" curiosity seekers and plunderers alike swarmed the beach. Some offered help to the crew. Others, bobbing about the surf in small rowboats, stripped copper from the ship's hull and carried away valuable cargo.

Many camped on the bluffs nearby, feasting on food from the ship's larder. "There was an abundance of much that was good to eat and drink. Long handled shovels were excellent frying pans," a scavenger mused. "The menu, though of no great variety, was a surprise — bacon, ham, fresh eggs brought round the Horn in lime water, beans, coffee, hard tack, sweet cakes, and preserves in unlimited quantity."

On June 8th the steamer *Active* was dispatched to salvage the *Carrier Pigeon's* payload.

The *Active* was diverted to the scene while en route to the Farallon Islands, sixty miles northwest of Pigeon Point, with the U.S. Marshall to remove squatters who laid claim to the area's lighthouse property.

It was common practice, and maritime law decreed, that the first salvage ship or "wrecker" to reach a stranded vessel claimed its cargo and sold it at auction for the ship owner. Wreckers received a portion of the profits from the sale or were paid a fee by the ship owner. Any delay in recovering cargo meant costly losses for ship owner and wrecker alike.

The *Active's* good intentions were thwarted by bickering over salvage rights. Apparently, the *Carrier Pigeon's* captain, Azariah Doane, had misgivings about the *Active's* recovery operation. "If Captain Doane had not had unfounded fears of salvage claims and had accepted the

Salvagers took advantage of the wreck of the Carrier Pigeon, *just as they did in the East Coast scene pictured above.* Harper's New Monthly Magazine.

offered aid of the steamer *Active*," one bystander complained, "he might have saved the new ship and its cargo."

According to another account, "If the parties interested had allowed the *Active* to go to work, without bartering and bantering on salvage, a considerable amount of property might have been saved for the underwriters." The *Active* remained nearby until the arrival of another vessel, the *Sea Bird*.

The "ever punctual steamer," *Sea Bird*, arrived June 9th. Built at New York in 1850 for the profitable California coastal trade, the 444-ton sidewheeler came to the *Carrier Pigeon*'s aid from San Francisco. Unfortunately, within thirty-six hours the *Sea Bird* met with her own mishap only feet away from the helpless *Carrier Pigeon*.

The *Sea Bird* was lying at anchor astern of the *Carrier Pigeon* when heavy swells snapped her anchor chains and anchor, pitching her onto the rocks. In minutes, the steamer began filling with water. With decks awash and all hands frantically pumping the bilges, the captain ordered the ship beached to save her from sinking.

"Bully" Arrives

On June 11th, Capt. Robert Waterman, commanding the 333-ton steamer *Goliah*, arrived to bring order to the chaos and to save as much cargo as possible. A notorious ship master, Capt. Waterman had earned the moniker of "Bully" after being charged with brutality on the clipper *Challenge*.

Born in New York in 1808, Waterman first went to sea at age twelve on a vessel bound for China. Throughout his career, Waterman attracted attention for his efficiency and ability to maintain order and discipline among passengers and crew. He even became something of a hero, rescuing a sailor who fell overboard from aloft during a gale.

In July of 1851, in spite of having difficulty assembling a crew, and expressing his intention to retire from the sea, Waterman took command of the clipper *Challenge*. During the trip around Cape Horn, mutiny broke out and drastic measures were taken to enforce order and obedience.

When the ship finally arrived in San Francisco, crew members alleged that "Five seamen were beaten and kicked to death, four others had been deliberately shaken from the rigging, and five more, mangled and maimed, still lay on the ship." A mob demanded that Waterman be turned over for hanging or burning.

Capt. Robert "Bully" Waterman had a reputation as a hard driving ship captain. He was also instrumental in naming Pigeon Point. The Mariners' Museum.

At his own request, Waterman stood trial. He was exonerated and settled in California, but the debate continued, even after his death in 1884. To some, he was "Captain Bob," a hard worker and conscientious master. To others, he was "Bully" Waterman, a brute and a murderer.

Controversy over Waterman's reputation hindered the *Goliah*'s rescue effort. "He attempted to enforce upon the boys the overbearing dictum of the experience of his shipmasters' tyrannical manners and mode," one salvager snorted.

Whatever the truth may be, Waterman's salvage terms for the *Carrier Pigeon* were generous for himself. He wanted all unbroken and uninjured articles and packages. Other wreckers could have everything else. The *Goliah* took the crews from the *Carrier Pigeon* and the *Sea Bird* to San Francisco, then returned to remove freight and machinery from both ships. Most of the cargo between decks, part of it damaged, was recovered. Ultimately, over 1,200 packages of merchandise were saved.

A Final Testament

Flung across the jagged rocks, the *Carrier Pigeon* and the *Sea Bird* lay like forlorn gulls with broken wings. Over the next six months the *Sea Bird* was repaired and resumed her coastal service. In 1857, the little ship survived a massive tidal wave caused by an earthquake, only to burn to the waterline off Discovery Island, Canada a year later.

The *Carrier Pigeon* was even less fortunate. According to the underwriters notice, "The ship then being full of water, her back broken, is momentarily expected to go to pieces, being exposed to the full force of the surf which beat over her." Within days, the once graceful clipper ship splintered and sank slowly from sight.

Some said the vessel was so beaten by the roaring surf that a piece of the ship's gilded figurehead washed ashore. If so, its whereabouts is unknown. The *Carrier Pigeon*'s only remaining remnant is the ship's bell, now in the hands of a private collector.

The incident was so unforgettable that two versions exist regarding the naming of the site where the *Carrier Pigeon* wrecked. According to one story, when the next shipload of locally grown potatoes reached San Francisco, someone reported that it was arriving from Carrier Pigeon Point. Before long, the name was shortened to Pigeon Point.

The ship's bell of the clipper Carrier Pigeon. Jeff Parry.

The other account insists that the point was named by Capt. Waterman and an unknown resident. According to this story, in sending a letter to his principals in San Francisco, Waterman inquired about the site's identity. "I told him it had none but said it was in the neighborhood of New Year's Point," the resident recalled.

"To this he objected and proposed dating his letter from Carrier Pigeon Point. Deeming this title good enough but somewhat lengthy, I proposed he drop the Carrier and call the point Pigeon Point," the man continued. "This satisfied the captain and it was so named."

In either case, it was through the *Carrier Pigeon*'s misfortune that she gained immortality.

2

ORDINARY SEAMEN, EXTRAORDINARY SOULS

JANUARY 17, 1865

Bold, adventurous, and ill-fated, the *Sir John Franklin* collided with destiny at Pigeon Point on January 17, 1865. All that remains is a near-forgotten cemetery, a poignant reminder of the dangers of seafaring.

Liverpool Packet

The *Sir John Franklin*, like the famed English explorer whose name she bore, had her fair share of adventure. The 171-foot clipper was built at Baltimore, Maryland in 1854 by John J. Abrams & Sons, a well known shipbuilder in the Fells Point District of that city from 1841 to 1867.

She served first as one of the Mankin Line packets. In the early 1840s, there were no regular shipping lines between Baltimore, Maryland and Liverpool, England. Vessels came and went in a random manner with no scheduled sailing dates. In 1848, Henry Mankin established a liner service with ships adapted to passenger, as well as freight traffic, sailing at established times.

Known as the "Liverpool Packets," the line prospered for twenty years. Demand for North American timber and cotton as raw materials for British industry led to a well-established transatlantic trade.

11

When steam began replacing sail on the North Atlantic run, the clipper Sir John Franklin *was sent to the Pacific in search of cargoes.* San Mateo County History Museum.

Immigrants from the British Isles and mainland Europe, along with British manufactured goods, provided a useful return cargo.

"Each vessel brought several hundred immigrants who were distributed along the street in groups awaiting wagons to convey them to the railroad stations," reported the *Baltimore Sun*.

"It was a pleasure for Mr. Mankin that he was enabling strong, healthy men and women to find good homes in this country where their work was needed."

The *Sir John Franklin* and other ships involved in the demanding packet trade made regular transatlantic voyages year round. Depending on the weather, passages could be as fast as twenty days or as slow as fifty or more, outbound from Baltimore. The return voyage from Liverpool could be even longer, and no doubt more trying, during winter months. No matter how light or heavy the cargo, human or otherwise, the Liverpool packets maintained their schedule and became a mainstay of the sailing industry.

In the 1860s, steam started to replace sail on the transatlantic route. With the gradual loss of the sailing packet market, Mankin sought broader opportunities. The *Sir John Franklin* was pressed into service to meet more promising commercial needs on the Pacific Coast.

On the first leg of her final journey to San Francisco, the *Sir John Franklin,* under the command of Capt. John Despeau, stopped in Rio de Janeiro. There, the clipper took on unexpected cargo from the *Charles L. Pennell*. Bound for San Francisco from New York, the *Charles L. Pennell* put into port in distress and was later condemned. The cargo of dry goods, lumber, pianos, and 300 barrels of spirits subsequently carried by the *Sir John Franklin* from the *Charles L. Pennell* was insured for $350,000.

Along with the surplus cargo, Capt. Despeau took on an extra hand, Robert Dawson Owens, a supercargo. Typically, the supercargo was a person appointed by the owners of the cargo to manage all the commercial aspects of the voyage, in particular the sale and purchase of goods. In this instance, Owens was a representative of the firm handling the sale and disposition of goods from the *Charles L. Pennell*.

The *Sir John Franklin* carried nineteen other crew, including seamen Edward J. Church, John Devine, Charles Martin, John Sooltine, and Jacob Staten. Church was only sixteen years old.

A Seaman's Life

Ordinary seamen, like Church, were extraordinary souls, for a

Whether an experienced able-bodied seaman or a boy apprentice, sailors were ex-pected to serve as helmsmen as part of their duties. U.S. Lighthouse Society.

sailor's life during the era of sail was exceptionally harsh. The seaman faced danger, deprivation, and a daily grind of rigorous labor. Yet, many eagerly went to sea.

Usually, a boy apprenticed himself at about age twelve, serving two or three years before becoming an ordinary seaman. The next step up the ladder was able-bodied seaman. Annual pay rates for able seamen were around $18 a month, for ordinary seamen $12, and as little as $8 for boys.

Even on "a first class ship" such as the *Sir John Franklin*, the living environment was miserably cramped. At her broadest point the clipper was only 36 feet wide. And since most of the 999-ton vessel carried the precious cargo, seamen's quarters were confined to the forecastle, or "fo'c'sle," a small, below-deck area in the bow of the ship. In this meager space, a seaman slept on a tiny slatted bunk with barely enough room for clothes and keepsakes from home. "It wasn't no castle," one old salt proclaimed.

A variety of vittles might be eaten for breakfast, lunch, or dinner, including salt pork or salt beef, bean soup, boiled rice, bread with molasses, coffee, and always plenty of sea biscuit or hardtack. Other concoctions were scouse, a beef hash mixed with potatoes or biscuits, and pease, a dried portable soup considered as an acceptable substitute for fresh vegetables. Along with the usual ration of grog, a steamed flour pudding called "duff" was savored in the evening.

During the voyage, Church and each of his mates were expected to stand as helmsman, steering the ship under the orders of an officer. Another primary duty was reefing, or shortening, sails by ropes called reef lines, to reduce the area of sail exposed to the wind. All mariners agreed, "Competent knowledge of steering, reefing, and furling makes a sailor."

By far, the most hazardous job was furling, for it meant taking in sail when the weather was at its worst. Seamen scrambled up into wet, swaying rigging and out onto slippery yards to gather up billowing canvas, punch it into shape, and lash it down. On a ship like the *Sir John Franklin*, which carried more sail than most other clippers of the day, the task was especially dangerous.

Church and his shipmates faced other perils. Aboard a frequently pitching, heaving vessel, with heavy rigging, shifting cargoes, and unpredictable weather and seas, physical injuries were all too common. Maladies such as dysentery, consumption, pleurisy, anemia, and scurvy were constant threats. "A sailor's life at best is a mixture of a little good

The most hazardous job for seamen was furling, for it meant taking in sail when the weather was at its worst. The Mariners' Museum.

with much evil," author Richard Henry Dana wrote, "and a little pleasure with much pain."

And then, there was the ever-present risk of shipwreck.

Disaster

On the misty evening of January 17, 1865, fearing that the *Sir John Franklin* was entering breakers, First Officer Boyd roused Capt. Despeau from his sleep. Due to thick fog, navigation readings hadn't been taken for over twenty-four hours. Yet, according to the captain's reckoning, the vessel was "far out to sea." Believing his ship to be seventy miles from shore, Capt. Despeau had unwittingly headed inland.

From the deck came the lookout's cry, "Breakers ahead!" Immediately, Capt. Despeau gave the order to "wear ship." A dangerous maneuver, he was attempting to run with the wind by quickly turning the vessel's stern through the wind in a sharp U-turn. Desperately, the clipper fought to gain open water, but the fury of the sea proved overwhelming. The vessel crashed brutally against the rocks. The first blow punctured a large hole in the hull. The second and third strikes broke the ship in half, spilling cargo and crew into the treacherous surf.

"She struck with great violence on the rocks, staving her bottom, and carrying her masts overboard," First Officer Boyd stated later. "In a few minutes, the vessel parted amidships and all was terror and confusion."

After two grueling hours of struggling through dark, frigid water, First Officer Boyd, Second Officer Ball, Third Officer Welch, and five unnamed seamen gained the shore. Sadly, the strong undertow carried Capt. Despeau, Seaman Church, and the rest of the crew out to sea. "This is the second ship lost at the same point," local newspapers later declared, "and is by far the most disastrous shipwreck which has ever happened on our coast."

Wet, cold, and exhausted, survivors wandered the shore for several more hours before reaching the safety of a farm house. "They were hospitably cared for, every attention being paid to them," a resident disclosed. "In the morning the neighbors came to bring relief with clothing, and kindly furnished Mr. Boyd with means of conveyance to the city."

Hoping to salvage some of the cargo, the *Sir John Franklin*'s owners dispatched a sheriff and six policemen to the scene. "Everything is a confused mass of boxes and barrels," newspapers reported. "Hundreds of men are gathering in the floating packages of clothes, liquors, and pianos, all in damaged condition save the barreled liquids."

After the Sir John Franklin *foundered, a stone monument was erected in memory of the lost crew.* San Mateo County History Museum.

Sharp-eyed beachcombers also picnicked on tins of turkey, chicken, oysters, and fruit found embedded in the sand. If driftwood was too wet, fires were easily made from cans of coal oil bobbing in the surf. Occasionally, sharp explosions echoed from the beach. It was merely a greenhorn who'd forgotten to punch a hole in the can before warming it in the fire.

Curiously, dozens of the 300 barrels of spirits listed on the ship's manifest disappeared. Eventually, 200 casks of whiskey were recovered and later sold in San Francisco. Some eager buyers complained that their kegs had been tampered with and refilled with saltwater. Apparently, many had been drained by thirsty coastside residents.

Remembered Still

The *Sir John Franklin*'s salt-scoured quarterboard, or nameplate, washed ashore and was saved by a local farmer. For nearly a century, the memento hung in a barn. Today, it is part of the archives of the San Francisco Maritime National Historical Park.

The bodies of two officers and four seamen were recovered also. Although the crew of the *Sir John Franklin* hailed from different parts of the globe, they all recognized the ranking system of a ship at sea. In death, accordingly, they were buried based on that status.

The remains of Capt. John Despeau of Baltimore and Supercargo Robert Dawson Owens of New York were taken to San Francisco and buried at Lone Mountain Cemetery. Years later the cemetery was abandoned and many of the bodies were deposited in a mass grave at Cypress Lawn Cemetery.

Seamen John Devine of England, Charles Martin of Norway, John Sooltine and Jacob Staten, both of Finland, were buried on a sandy bluff near the site of the wreck. The site, today called Franklin Point, is part of Año Nuevo State Reserve. A stone monument, now missing, was erected in memory of Edward J. Church and other lost crew.

Over the years, strong winds eroded sand dunes covering the graves. In 1980, an unsuspecting hiker discovered exposed human remains. Archeological work in the area uncovered four redwood coffins two years later. Most likely, they are the coffins of the four seamen buried at the point after the wreck of the *Sir John Franklin*. Their bones have since been re-interred and rest protected from further intrusion.

Though shrouded by the sands of time, the crew of the *Sir John Franklin*, their toil, and their sacrifice are remembered still.

Through the years, storms uncovered the coffins and remains of four seamen from the Sir John Franklin *buried near Pigeon Point.* San Mateo County History Museum.

3

From Darkness Into Light

November 24, 1866
November 18, 1868

Within bowshot of where the *Sir John Franklin* sank, both the *Coya* and the *Hellespont* met identical fates. The tragedies spurred an outcry so fervent that Pigeon Point was transformed forever.

Sailing Ships and Shovels

In the 1860s, barks like the *Coya* and the *Hellespont* were used as colliers to deliver coal from Australian mines. Ships from Australia could arrive in Pacific ports faster than those from the North Atlantic, which had to sail down and then up the length of South America.

Perched atop vast natural deposits of lignite and bituminous ore, Australia was, and still is, one of the largest coal producers in the world. This "black gold," a reliable energy source for hundreds of years, was an important fuel for California's growing cities and industries.

Two primary Australian ports, Sydney and Newcastle, were the earliest to take advantage of the abundant coal deposits dotting their shores. Founded as penal colonies, the settlements relied on convict labor to mine the ore. In 1799, coal became Australia's first commercial export cargo.

Similar to the vessels shown above loading at Newcastle, the Coya *and the* Hellespont *were used as colliers to deliver coal from Australia's vast ore deposits.* State Library of Victoria.

In the 1860s, ships from Australia delivered coal to Pacific ports in a shorter time than those that came from the eastern seaboard. Bancroft Library.

First known as Port Jackson, Sydney was established in 1788 with over 1,000 male and female convicts, marines, assorted officials, and their families. Although free settlers began arriving in Sydney in 1793, the transport of convicts wasn't abolished until 1840.

The first harbor master was appointed in 1811 to control the growing port.

Newcastle, or Kings Town, was settled in 1801. A coal mine was soon established, but within a year prisoners mutinied and the site was abandoned. Little wonder, since coal was mined through tedious, backbreaking toil. Using only shovels, convicts dug holes into nearby cliffs to extract the inky rock by hand. In 1804 the area was resettled and renamed Newcastle. By the 1860s, Newcastle was a key shipping and commercial center.

Originally, the coal was moved from huge piles dumped near the dock and loaded onto the vessels using shovels and wheelbarrows. It wasn't until 1831 that coal was loaded by mechanical means for the first time. The process became more efficient in 1860 when steam cranes were introduced. A free-flowing bulk cargo, the coal was poured directly into the holds of the ships.

All to No Avail

The *Coya*, built in 1863 by Dudgeo at London, England, was consigned to Australia's Macondray & Company in 1865. The vessel had a length of 156 feet and measured 515 tons. The bark's hull was composed of metal plates less than an inch thick. The slender iron hull created more room for cargo, was more economical to maintain, leaked less, and was less susceptible to fire than a wooden one.

Unfortunately, the *Coya's* durable hull could not make her immune to difficulties on her last crossing. Twelve days out of Sydney, seaman Peter Johnson fell off the jib boom and drowned. Many thought this a dreadful omen. The mishap, however, did nothing to deter James Martin, an eager young stowaway hoping to join the ship's ranks.

On the day she wrecked, the *Coya* carried twenty-nine passengers and crew. Blinded by steel gray skies filled with heavy mist, plagued by forceful winds and heavy seas, the meandering bark labored up the shadowy California coast. Days before the disaster, unable to take reliable readings or soundings, the captain depended on "dead reckoning" to navigate. This consisted of running the last reliable position up to the present, allowing for projected effects of currents and weather.

Among the travelers were six women, including the captain's wife and daughter. Most were below deck enjoying tea when the ship splintered like reeds. "The sea kept lifting her from rock to rock, crushing in the bottom," George Byrnes, a passenger recalled. "With the sea breaking over us, nothing could be seen but a mass of hissing foam."

Amid the ensuing chaos, Capt. H. Paige struggled courageously to save his family, passengers, and crew. Dr. Rowden gallantly cast off his life vest and lashed it to his wife.

Protectively, Mrs. Jeffreys bundled her baby into a woolen shawl. Someone offered a prayer. "All was to no avail," Byrnes murmured. "The ladies were screaming and being washed away one by one."

The only survivors were George Byrnes, First Mate Thomas Barstow, and Seaman Walter Cooper. Cooper reached land by "clinging to a piece of timber with death's grip."

The others bobbled ashore wearing cork life belts. Badly bruised and beaten, the trio spent a miserable night huddled together in a hole in the sand.

At daylight, they made their way to a nearby rancho. The scene upon their return was grim. The *Coya's* hull had disappeared entirely.

The beach was strewn with fragments of the wreck, including Dr. Rowden's travel chest. One body, that of Mrs. Jeffreys, lay among the ship's remains, her empty, tattered shawl nearby.

"That coast is a very dangerous one, on account of the peculiar location, climate, and currents," the coroner's investigation and jury's report on the *Coya's* disaster concluded, "It seems to be very evident that it is the duty of the proper authorities to put a light on the point."

It was yet another lonely cry for help.

"No Loss and Great Gain"

Unlike the *Coya*, the *Hellespont* was constructed of sturdy oak. The bark had a length of 160 feet, a beam of 32 feet, and measured 750 tons. Built at Bath, Maine in 1856 by E. & A. Sewall, the vessel was owned by N.L. & G. Griswold of New York. The *Hellespont's* builder and owner were both distinguished merchants of the day.

The Sewall family was influential in Bath commerce from the 1820s, when William Sewall established a shipping yard. In 1854, his sons formed E. & A. Sewall, changing the venture's name to Arthur Sewall & Company in 1879. The enterprise was one of the first to build

The N.L. & G. Griswold Co. house flag was a blue-and-white checkerboard. Publisher's collection.

and operate square-rigged steel-hulled sailing ships, and constructed the last square-rigger produced on the East Coast.

Founded in 1822, N.L. & G. Griswold was another prominent firm. Beginning with West Indies routes, Nathaniel Lynde Griswold and his brother, George, created a profitable shipping company. They branched out into the China tea trade, and, later, into supporting California gold rush markets. The company initials, N.L. & G.G., were said to stand for "no loss and great gain." Unluckily, the motto lacked enough power to keep the *Hellespont* afloat.

Outbound from Newcastle, New South Wales, when she foundered, the vessel carried 1,100 tons of coal and eighteen crew. Like the *Coya* two years before, the *Hellespont* had sailed for days in fierce seas and inclement weather. "We ran directly in among the breakers," helmsman Frederick Wilson declared. "She struck once, heavily, bows on, and then swung broadsides onto the rocks."

The men began scrambling on deck from below. "For God's sake come out," the First Mate cried, "or we shall be ashore!" Capt. Cornelius Soule, regarded by his crew as "a trustworthy man and skilled navigator," grabbed an axe and began cutting away the masts. The next instant, a tremendous wave struck the ship and split her in two. Planks and spars smashed apart, littering the water's surface. The entire crew was thrust into the churning surf. "The sea nearly buried me," Wilson, one of the few survivors, reflected.

"Sometimes, I could hear the cries of my shipmates in the water about me. One after another, the cries stopped."

Flailing about in surging whitecaps, a stunned seaman, George Thomas, and the injured Capt. Soule caught a piece of wreckage. "Captain, you were a little nearer land than you thought," Thomas commented. "Yes, but it was not my fault," Capt. Soule replied. "I did the best I could."

THIS DAY.

TUESDAY.....................November 24, 1868

At 1 O'clock P. M.

At the New Merchants' Exchange
California Street,

For account underwriters—

WE WILL SELL

THE AMERICAN SHIP
 **HELLESPONT,**

As She Now Lies, near Pescadero,

TOGETHER WITH

Her Sails, Rigging, Anchors, Chains
Cargo of Coal, Etc.

TERMS CASH

JONES & BENDIXEN,
Auctioneers.

no24

As this wreck sale notice shows, the wreck of the Hellespont *was sold for salvage.*
Author's collection.

Drenched and numb with cold, Thomas, Wilson, and other survivors crawled up a bluff and stumbled upon a trail leading to the whaling station at Pigeon Point.

Unhappily, Capt. Soule and ten of his crew were not among the desolate troop. "The people rendered them every assistance," accounts said, "and furnished them with dry clothes, food, drink, and warm comfortable beds."

At a prayer meeting in the fishermen's chapel in Pescadero, the *Hellespont's* survivors offered thanks for having been spared. "Tearfully," one resident recounted, "they mourned the sad fate of their officers and shipmates, so suddenly torn away from the companionship of the living, and whelmed in the cold abyss of the pitiless sea."

A Public Outcry

Though silenced by the sea, those lost aboard the *Coya* and the *Hellespont* were not forgotten. The magnitude of the combined tragedies generated an impassioned public outcry. H.A. Scofield, editor of the *San Mateo County Gazette*, was particularly ardent.

"The recent terrible wreck of the ship, *Hellespont*, at Pigeon Point which resulted in the loss of eleven of her crew, including Captain Soule, constitutes another appeal to the government at Washington for the establishment of a lighthouse at Pigeon Point," Scofield wrote.

"Pigeon Point is the most extensive promontory on the coast south of the Golden Gate, and the point seems especially adapted for a lighthouse. No other place on the Pacific Coast has proved so fatal to navigators as this locality," he stressed. "Several vessels have been wrecked in that vicinity within the past few years and many lives have been lost."

A lighthouse was not the only aid to navigation regarded as helpful in warning mariners against the dangers of Pigeon Point's coast. In dense fog, a light alone would provide little safety for mariners. "A fog bell or whistle would unquestionably be found useful," Scofield urged. "A bell or whistle of sufficient volume at Pigeon Point would have saved the *Hellespont* and other vessels which have been lost in the vicinity."

The editor encouraged those interested in maritime affairs to bring their influence to bear upon government officials, and "never relax their effort" until a lighthouse was erected at Pigeon Point. "Our delegates in Congress are expected to make it their business to look after this matter," he insisted, "and they should not be permitted to forget the influence of their constituents."

Scofield was not alone in his commentary. For the previous decade, the U.S. Lighthouse Board had been under constant attack by shippers, navigators, and chambers of commerce across the country. All complained of the inadequate lighthouse system. Beleaguered by internal politics, the Board was slow in overcoming its deficiencies and placing emphasis on new lighthouse locations.

Finally, Scofield and others exerted enough pressure on the Lighthouse Board to build a fog signal station and lighthouse at Pigeon Point. At the end of 1868, Congress appropriated $90,000 for the purpose, and two years later the site was purchased. In 1871, the fog signal went into service.

On November 15, 1872, Pigeon Point Lighthouse first displayed its brilliant beam across the dark waters.

The loss of the Coya *and the* Hellespont, *along with the death of thirty-seven passengers and crew, stirred a public outcry that resulted in a lighthouse at Pigeon Point.* Author's collection.

4

A BAD YEAR AT NEW YEAR'S POINT

APRIL 10, 1887
DECEMBER 20, 1887

Two disastrous shipwrecks punctuated 1887. The *J.W. Seaver* and the *San Vicente* met their ends due to peculiar accidents near Año Nuevo Point, just five miles south of Pigeon Point. The combined mishaps took fifteen lives. The two ships were lost forever.

Chert and Cheese

Spanish mariners began charting California's coast in the 1600s. One of them, Sebastian Vizcaino, discovered a low, foggy, windswept peninsula on January 3, 1603. The diarist and chaplain for that expedition, Father Antonio de la Ascension, christened the promontory Punta de Año Nuevo, or New Year's Point.

At the time, inhabitants called Quiroste lived in the area, harvesting fish and shellfish for food. These Native Californians are known today as the Ohlone. In addition to hunting and fishing, they collected "chert" from the beach to make arrow points, knives, scrapers, spear points, and other tools. A lustrous blue-gray rock resembling flint and consisting of crystalline quartz, chert was also a valuable trade item.

Europeans reappeared in 1769 when Gaspar de Portola, a Spanish soldier and explorer, led an overland expedition from San Diego to

Año Nuevo, or New Year's Point, is located five miles south of Pigeon Point. U.S. Coast Guard.

San Francisco. Since then, Año Nuevo, roughly nine acres in size, has had many owners and many uses. After being used as pastureland by missionaries, the parcel became a private rancho in 1842. In 1861, a subsequent owner sold land adjacent to Año Nuevo to the Steele Brothers.

Along with their cousin, Rensselaer, the industrious Steeles had established eleven dairies in three counties by 1867. The rapid expansion was due primarily to the popularity of the cheese they produced. According to family lore, Rensselaer's wife, Clara, "persuaded them to rope and milk some of the wild Spanish cattle, and using a recipe she found, made some cheese." It must have been pretty savory fare. Their dairy operations continued for eighty years.

Año Nuevo was also the site of a fog signal station and lighthouse. After the wreck of the *Carrier Pigeon* in 1853, the Lighthouse Board surveyed the surrounding area for possible lighthouse locations. Surveyors considered a station on Año Nuevo Island, which was connected to the mainland by a sandbar at low tide, and on Año Nuevo Point, which was more accessible, at a higher elevation, and more stable. In 1857, plans were developed for a lighthouse at Año Nuevo Point but never executed. Difficulties acquiring land and the outbreak of the Civil War delayed further progress.

In 1872, when Pigeon Point Lighthouse was built, a fog signal station with a steam whistle was also placed at Año Nuevo Point. A keeper's dwelling was constructed at the southern end of Año Nuevo Island, with a wooden walkway running north to the fog signal station. Travel between the two areas proved risky. In 1882, two keepers and two visitors were washed out to sea while leaving the island.

A lighthouse of sorts was erected at Año Nuevo Point in 1890. The light was merely a lens lantern mounted on a water tank. Around 1906, a two-story duplex was built next to the original keeper's dwelling. Eventually, a skeleton tower with a Fresnel lens in the lantern room was constructed in 1916.

The station was deactivated in 1948, and replaced by a whistle buoy that is still operating.

A Hard-Working Cargo Ship

Built at Somerville, Massachusetts in 1859, the *J. W. Seaver's* beginning was promising enough. Somerville, located just north of Boston, is the historic location of the first ship built in the American colonies.

The 230-ton bark spent her initial years dedicated to the flourishing New England-West Indies trade. Ships like the *J.W. Seaver* ventured often to the West Indies with goods such as butter, fish, flour, and timber. They returned fully laden with exotic payloads of mahogany, molasses, indigo, and rum.

Owned by Andrew Crawford and Company of San Francisco, the *J.W. Seaver* sailed around Cape Horn in 1863 to enter a career in California's bustling coastal trade. As a small, hardworking, cargo ship, she called on innumerable West Coast ports, delivering tons of freight — foodstuffs, farming supplies, household supplies, lumber mill equipment — each year. Stripped, scraped, and caulked, the resolute bark put to sea time and time again. The aging vessel was bound for Astoria, Oregon from Santa Cruz, twenty-seven miles south of Pigeon Point, carrying a cargo of sixty tons of hay and ten tons of salt, when she wrecked.

On April 10, 1887, just a day out of Santa Cruz, Capt. Robert Robertson noticed that the ship was leaking. Years of slapdash repairs had finally taken their toll. Although the crew worked incessantly, keeping at the pumps for more than twelve hours, the *J.W. Seaver* was sinking. With the lee side of the deck under water, the captain headed for the beach at Año Nuevo.

"A strong wind was blowing and a heavy surf was rolling in, breaking over the ship fore and aft," Capt. Robertson declared. "We attempted to launch a boat but it was immediately smashed to atoms. Nothing more could be done but to take our chances and get ashore on pieces of the vessel."

With waves as high as thirty feet crashing around them, local ranchers, including the Steele brothers, braved the breakers to rescue the struggling crew. Tying ropes to their waists, the men formed a human chain into the sea, dragging survivors from the undertow. Five of the eight crew, among them Capt. Robertson, were saved.

Unluckily, Second Officer John Moore and Seaman Eduard Samuelson drowned when planks from the broken bark slipped from their grasp. The ship's cook, frantic with fear, never left the deck.

About a hundred yards from the water's edge floated what was left of the *J.W. Seaver.* Only a lone, jagged remnant of the bow protruded from the swirling surf. Spars, sails, and rigging lay in a tangled mass ashore. Countless bales of hay and splintered timbers littered the beach for half a mile. Among the debris lay the ship's large iron water tank. Valued at $10,000, the bark was a total loss.

"That she was an old vessel could be plainly seen from the rotten condition of the planks and timbers scattered about," the *Santa Cruz Daily Surf* reported. "She evidently was a rotten old hulk and should have been condemned long ago." It was a sad epitaph for a venerable vessel.

Tragedy at the Winter Solstice

The *San Vicente* was another hard-working little ship. Built in 1875 for the Reis Brothers of San Francisco, she was designed for the coast's brisk lime trade. Serving many of the same busy ports as the *J.W. Seaver*, no doubt the routes of the two vessels crossed many times.

Drawn to California during the Gold Rush, the four Reis brothers prospered through freighting and mercantile activities. One of their ventures was the Santa Cruz Lime Company. Lime, used for mortar, plaster, and whitewash, was an important part of the booming building industry. Santa Cruz was an ideal location for their enterprise. Redwood, used for fueling limekilns and making barrels to store and transport lime, and labor supplied by unemployed men from the gold fields, were readily available. The bay also afforded convenient means of shipping the finished product to market.

Unfortunately, competition proved too formidable for the Reis Brothers. Three larger operations, Davis & Cowell, IXL, and W.T. Holmes, soon produced the bulk of lime used in San Francisco and throughout the state. In 1876, the *San Vicente* was sold to the Pacific Coast Steamship Company.

The Pacific Coast Steamship Company grew out of the successful partnership of Charles and Edwin Goodall, Christopher Nelson, and

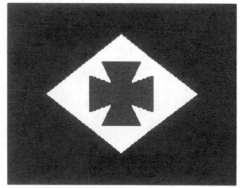

The house flag of the Pacific Coast Steamship Co. consisted of a red maltese cross in a white diamond on a blue background. Publisher's collection.

A bird's eye view of Santa Cruz, a busy port visited often by cargo ships such as the J.W. Seaver *and the* San Vicente. Bancroft Library.

The San Vicente *made scores of trips along California's coast for
the Pacific Coast Steamship Co.* David F. Myrick Collection.

George Perkins. Prominent local businessmen, they bought a secondhand steamer in 1874 and placed it on the San Francisco to San Diego route. The vessel made the run in record time.

Swiftly, the group acquired a fleet of wooden, propeller-driven ships, including the *San Vicente*, all under 1,000 gross tons. Most of the vessels were chartered from small operators, furnishing service to more than twenty ports scattered along the California coast.

After reorganizing their growing concern, Goodall, Nelson, and Perkins created the Pacific Coast Steamship Company.

One of the firm's promotional pamphlets boasted, "Freight consigned to this company promptly forwarded." Apparently, the enterprise delivered what it promised. Although Goodall, Nelson, and Perkins sold controlling interest to the Oregon Improvement Company in 1881, the Pacific Coast Steamship Company remained a dominant firm in coastal traffic for forty years.

Traveling unceasingly, the *San Vicente* made scores of trips up and down the coast. She proved to be a "lucky ship" for her new owners, never losing a dollar through all her years of service. Possibly because of this, the steamer, valued at $30,000, carried no insurance. The 246-ton vessel was bound for Santa Cruz from San Francisco when disaster struck near Año Nuevo Point. She carried forty-five tons of cargo, mostly holiday merchandise consigned to shop owners in Santa Cruz, and empty lime barrels.

The evening of December 20, 1887 was clear and starlit with strong north-by-northwest winds. Shortly before 7:00 P.M., First Officer Charles Green sighted smoke in the engine room. Hoping to reach the fire, the crew cleared away the main hatch. They succeeded only in causing a strong draft which sent flames bursting skyward. Below decks, empty lime barrels acted as kindling, spreading the blaze throughout the hold.

After another failed attempt to reach the hold and douse the fire, Capt. Charles Lewis ordered the port lifeboat swung out and lowered. Ignoring orders from the captain, panic-stricken seamen leapt aboard, nearly swamping the skiff. First Officer Green, ordered into the starboard lifeboat to keep it clear of flames, was overtaken by the remaining crew. Dangerously overloaded, the dinghy flopped into the sea, flinging everyone overboard.

Capt. Lewis and Second Officer Charles Spratt were left stranded on the burning vessel. Jettisoning loose combustibles, they lashed boards and hatch covers together to form a raft. Miraculously, a lifeboat from a passing steamer appeared just as they contemplated their plunge off the

This is probably the last photo taken of the San Vicente *before she burned at sea.*
Marshall Collection.

After the San Vicente *caught fire, the* Queen of the Pacific *rescued some of her crew. The survivors watched the burning vessel sink.* San Francisco Maritime National Historical Park.

doomed ship. The *Queen of the Pacific,* a popular passenger steamer also owned by the Oregon Improvement Company, had sighted the blazing *San Vicente* and lowered lifeboats to search for survivors. Despite the steamer's valiant efforts, twelve of the *San Vicente*'s eighteen crew were lost. From the deck of the *Queen of the Pacific* a distraught Capt. Lewis noted, "We laid by the burning vessel until daylight and saw the wreck sink." Nothing remains of the *San Vicente*.

Her Pacific Coast Steamship Co. sister and helpmate, the *Queen of the Pacific*, foundered near San Luis Obispo Bay in 1888. When the engine room flooded with water, the stately ship limped 15 miles to shore and sank in shallow water. Fortunately, all passengers and crew escaped in lifeboats. Resurrected and towed to San Francisco, the vessel was renovated and renamed the *Queen*. But this was not the end of the steamer's misadventures. She burned at sea and was refurbished twice before joining the Admiral Line in 1916. The company provided a trans-Pacific service from 1917 to 1922, and was the largest coastal trade company on the Pacific Coast until 1938.

Echoes of the Past

In 1965, seventy-eight years after the *J.W. Seaver* wrecked, coastal resident Henry Bradley discovered a rusted bowsprit band, complete with deadeye, while strolling on the beach.

"It was just after a heavy storm and the surf had washed the sand away down to bedrock," he recalled. "That's where I found the piece of the ship." The iron relic resides in the archives of the San Francisco Maritime National Historical Park.

Still lonely, wild, and undeveloped, Año Nuevo Point today remains much as Sebastian Vizcaino saw it from his passing ship. The area, which became a state reserve in 1958, now comprises 1,200 acres of coastal land. Vestiges of the Steele Brothers Dairy, including old barns and other historic buildings, are still visible. Portions of the lighthouse tower, toppled in 1976 by the Coast Guard for safety reasons, lie strewn about. The keepers' residence stands in ruins, occupied now by sea birds and marine mammals.

Only the haunting barks of elephant seals protecting their young echo over this otherwise uninhabited area. Although, some say, when conditions are right, they can also hear the mournful ringing of two ships' bells.

5

MIXED SIGNALS, MISTAKEN BEARINGS

JULY 14, 1896

When the *Colombia* struck shore within a cable's length of Pigeon Point's tower, it was an inconvenience for her passengers. The only casualty was the exquisite steamer herself.

To the Wonder of All

Built in 1892 at Chester, Pennsylvania by Delaware River Shipbuilding, the *Colombia* was the newest steamer on the Pacific Mail Steamship Company's Panama route. The steel-hulled vessel had a length of 327 feet, a beam of 45 feet, and measured over 3,600 tons. Valued at $600,000, the *Colombia* carried ninety-two crew and sixty-two passengers.

The Pacific Mail Steamship Company, founded in 1848, was an esteemed shipping line for over seventy-five years. Corporate headquarters were in New York and the operating center in San Francisco. With the growing travel demands of California gold seekers, the firm began service between Panama and San Francisco in 1849.

Crossing Panama by land eliminated a months-long voyage of 15,000 miles around South America, but the journey remained strenuous. Passengers and mail were transported by ship from New

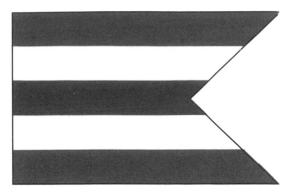

The house flag of Pacific Mail Steamship Co. was a burgee with blue stripes at top and bottom and a red stripe in the center. Publisher's collection.

York to Chagres on the eastern shore of the Isthmus of Panama. They were then conveyed south by mule across the Isthmus to Panama City, where ships picked them up for the trip to California. Steamers stopped in San Diego, Santa Barbara, Monterey, and San Francisco, completing a journey of less than 6,000 miles.

Within five years of its inception, Pacific Mail was running eighteen steamers and also inaugurated the first regular trans-Pacific steamship service. In 1855, the company's visionary founder, William Henry Aspinwall, completed construction of a railroad across Panama. The railroad offered the first service of its kind between the Atlantic and Pacific sides of the Isthmus.

Coordination of rail and steamship schedules resulted in a remarkable travel time of twenty-one days between New York and San Francisco. "The company's steamships demonstrate that they can accomplish more work at less cost than any steamer built," the firm boasted. "On the Panama route, that fact has been notorious, to the wonder of all experienced ship's masters and other experts."

As a result of its reputation for efficiency, dependability, and service, Pacific Mail flourished. Until completion of the transcontinental railroad in 1869, the company's vessels were the principal tie between the East and West Coasts. Pacific Mail remained active in both the Panama and trans-Pacific trades until 1925.

No Immediate Danger

In the 1890s, San Francisco was the most modern port in the United States, and the third largest by volume of ship traffic in the world. The *Colombia* offered a refined way to make the voyage. "Once on board, the traveler is shut off from all communication, with the world left behind," Pacific Mail's 1896 handbook professed. "The other travelers

The decks of the Pacific Mail Steamship Company's newest steamer, Colombia, *provided passengers with ample opportunity for leisure pursuits.* Author's collection.

Capt. William A. Clark, making his first trip as the Colombia*'s master, nearly drove the ship into Pigeon Point Lighthouse.* San Francisco Chronicle.

are pleasure bent, and among them one can find congenial friends in whose company the time will fly all too quickly."

According to one account, the *Colombia* "was as fine a coasting steamship as any flying the American flag." The vessel was fashionably decorated with satin drapery, marble tabletops, gilded furniture, silver serving ware, and ornate woodwork. Her three large decks provided ample opportunity for passengers to enjoy vigorous walking, amusing card games, or simply lounging, lost in the pages of the latest best-seller.

On this voyage the *Colombia's* last port was Acapulco, completing a series of picturesque tourist spots passengers enjoyed in Mexico. Nestled at the foot of a range of verdant hills, Acapulco's harbor was well-sheltered and ships could anchor close to shore. Pacific Mail had also established a supply station there for coal and provisions, as well as a transfer point for freight to vessels serving smaller ports down the coast.

On July 13, 1896, the evening before the *Colombia's* misfortune, the fog on the mid-California coast was so dense that it was impossible to see a hundred yards ahead. Capt. William A. Clark, making his first trip as the *Colombia's* master, stood watch throughout the night. Some speculated that, intent on setting a speed record, he kept the ship moving at a brisk 14 knots.

"The journey was made in thick, unpleasant fog. I had made the trip frequently enough to realize that full speed ahead under such conditions was inadvisable," Carlos B. Lastreto, a regular patron of the Pacific Mail Line observed. "However, I was just a passenger. It was none of my business that he was determined to break the existing speed record for the run."

When morning came, fog continued to hang over the coast like a vast gray blanket. Believing he had passed Pigeon Point, Capt. Clark turned eastward. Unfortunately, he ran onto the rocks just south of the point, nearly driving his ship into the lighthouse tower. A more humiliating conclusion to an elegant pleasure cruise is difficult to imagine. "It was a mistake in the fog horn signals," the captain sputtered. "We mistook that on Año Nuevo for the one at Pigeon Point and altered our course, thinking we had cleared the rocky cape."

Because sound waves reflect, fog signal equipment had its drawbacks. In "pea-soup" fog, it could be difficult for a ship's officer to tell exactly from what direction the sound was coming. When atmospheric conditions were just right, the sound could even bounce, so that a ship close to shore could not hear the signal, but one farther out to sea would.

The Colombia *struck shore and wedged fast on the rocks, suffering a 60-foot gash in her forward compartment.* San Mateo County History Museum.

"The fog signal must have been out of order," one of the ship's officers insisted. "It was as faint as if it were miles away, and it sounded far out at sea."

However, it seems unlikely that one fog signal could be mistaken for the other. Each had its own characteristic sound. Usually, ship officers identified these unique sounds by consulting a registry or list. "It was bad management," seasoned traveler Fred Donaldson declared. "The accident is one that clearly could have been avoided."

The *Colombia* struck within 150 yards of the beach. The impact sent only a slight ripple across the ship. Certainly, it was not enough to knock the steward out of his chair as he was having his shoes polished. Few were aware that the *Colombia* was wedged fast on the rocks, a gash sixty feet long in her forward compartment. "There was little confusion and no disorder from any quarter," eyewitness Lastreto stated. "The *Colombia* was resting securely on a reef, and there seemed no immediate danger."

Wilton Lackaye, an actor, was dressing when the *Colombia* struck. "I didn't feel the slightest bit alarmed. Neither did my wife," he remarked. Stepping out of the cabin, they encountered a young lady with her mother who inquired, "Is my hat straight?" There were no screams, not a faint, not a single prayer. Lackaye asserted, "I've seen more excitement at the ordinary shipboard fire drills."

As usual, passengers were called to breakfast by the steward's gong. Everyone went below as if nothing had happened, eagerly anticipating their morning coffee. For the remainder of the day, travelers spent their time as if leisurely at sea. Meals were served regularly, and the only anxiety anyone expressed was how long they might be delayed.

Limes and Lead Paint

The tugs *Active* and *Sea King* were dispatched to the *Colombia* from San Francisco to ferry passengers ashore. When help arrived around 10:00 P.M., the pampered travelers were reluctant to disembark. "We didn't know where we were," a Miss Tabor said. "We saw the boats ready to take us, but none of us wanted to go."

Passengers were removed as speedily as possible to the tugs' decks. Waving handkerchiefs and hats, voyagers gave three cheers in farewell to the ill-fated ship. Their one complaint: "Baggage was most indiscriminately piled on the deck."

As they departed, coastsiders quickly took advantage of the windfall afforded by the stranded ship. Tons of white lead were taken from the

The Sea King, *right, was one of the tugs dispatched to ferry the* Colombia*'s passengers ashore. The* Fearless, *center, helped with the final salvage.* San Francisco Maritime National Historical Park.

wreck, supplying every home with a fresh coat of paint. In addition, the *San Francisco Chronicle* revealed, "Hundreds of feet of white and gold molding secured from the staterooms of the steamer have been made into frames. Copper wire by the ton was taken and nearly every yard in the neighborhood has used it for clothes lines."

Also aboard the lame ship was a cargo of limes valued at $7,000. Fishermen avidly filled their boats to capacity, scooping up the tasty citrus bobbing about in the surf. Meanwhile, those afoot scurried along the shore snatching errant little orbs from the sand.

Zealously, Pacific Mail salvaged silverware, furniture, bedding, and most of the other foodstuffs. Schooners returned again and again for more of the estimated $250,000 cargo. In addition to 700 tons of general merchandise, there were 2,700 sacks of coffee, and hundreds of cases of cloth, Panama hats, fish oil, soap, canned sardines, and a decreasing number of limes.

The afflicted vessel became quite a tourist attraction. "She looks as if lying at anchor and there is no evidence to the eye that there is seventeen feet of water in her hold," the *San Francisco Examiner* noted. "She rests as she struck, heading northward for the peninsula which joins Pigeon Point to the foothills."

Sightseeing ships cruised off the coast allowing excursionists an opportunity to survey a shipwreck. Some tours included trips aboard the *Colombia* where curiosity seekers could forage for souvenirs. "Sunday was visiting day on board and not less than 500 people went off in small boats," the *Redwood City Democrat* reported a week after the grounding. "They spent an hour or more on board securing relics."

Wreckers took over, removing railing, bales of silks, cigars, dry goods, plumbing, and other hardware. Finally, under the supervision of the California Iron and Wrecking Company, the tugs *Fearless* and *Reliance* undertook removal of anything left of value aboard the fallen *Colombia*.

"She has been given up as a hopeless wreck. The jagged rocks off Pigeon Point have torn and mangled her beyond repair," newspapers reported. "The grinding and crunching of the steel plates of her hull can be heard for miles."

Not to Be Saved

Pigeon Point's Head Keeper, James Marner, served on many ships and viewed them with great sentiment. The veteran seaman sailed around

Cape Horn so many times he had lost count. Painfully, he watched the *Colombia* succumb to the sea.

At first, he had mistaken the *Colombia* for another ship. Thinking it was the tender *Madrona* making an impromptu visit with the lighthouse inspector aboard, he hollered to his crew. "They ran to put on their good clothes to receive the inspector, but we found our mistake. I could make out the *Colombia*," he recalled. "She was right up almost on dry land, and my fog horn blowing twice a minute all night. This is one of the queerest accidents I ever knew of, and I've been thirty-five years at sea."

Later, as she lay deserted and jammed against the rocks, Marner witnessed the ship's struggle to survive. "She was lifted by the roll of the sea and dropped again, into the rocks," he exclaimed. "She breathed out her life in great struggles with the waves."

Gradually, impaled by a huge rock thrust straight through her bow, over twenty-six feet of water seeped into the *Colombia*'s hold. Mercilessly, the sea whipped her around like a piece of driftwood. "Do you see how she fights for life? She won't let go of the rock," Marner mourned. "She's afraid of going down if she does. She thinks she'll hold on and live a little longer. But it's useless."

Looking down from the lighthouse tower, the keeper foretold the *Colombia*'s imminent demise. "You will never see her float again," he sighed. "Her time has come. She is not to be saved."

Left in ruins, the once grand vessel was dynamited three months later. Sadly, the *Colombia*'s loss was a case of mixed signals and mistaken bearings.

Pigeon Point Lighthouse's head keeper, James Marner, wistfully watched the Co-lombia *sink.* Frank Perry/Santa Cruz Public Library.

6

WORKHORSE
OF THE PACIFIC

AUGUST 9, 1913

A humble yet vital coastal schooner, the *Point Arena* was the mainstay of local maritime economy. One early morning, while dutifully loading her scheduled cargo, disaster struck.

"Dog Hole" Ports

For twenty-six years, the *Point Arena* served the California coast, hauling hundreds of tons of timber annually. The vessel called often at Pigeon Point, one of many tiny ports strung along the Pacific shores. Operating in these precarious coves was risky at best. A sudden gust of wind or errant swell could catch even the most stalwart ship by surprise.

Small harbors, such as Pigeon Point and other pocket bays along California's rugged coast, were nicknamed "dog hole" ports. Experienced sailors claimed the nickname grew out of the fact that there was "hardly room enough for a dog to turn around in one of those." Others said it came from the fact that each cove had a resident dog. Making their way up the coast in heavy fog, schooner captains navigated by memorizing each canine's distinctive bark.

Loading chutes, like this one at Pigeon Point (seen in an early stereopticon pho-tograph), were a common way to load cargo in small "dog hole" ports. Bancroft Library.

Although the stories are surely exaggerated, there is no doubt that working in these nooks was dangerous. It took great skill to maneuver in tight spaces in close proximity to rocky shores. And with no piers on which to tie their ships, captains awkwardly anchored their schooners bow out, oftentimes with their sterns in the surf.

In spite of Pigeon Point's semicircular bay being partially sheltered from northern winds, heavy swells rolling in from the southwest made a pier impractical. Lumber and tanbark, an essential ingredient for leather making, were loaded by chutes and slides, and later by long wires, extended from the craggy cliffs to the vessels anchored below.

Handling early chutes was fraught with risks. At the end of the chute stood a man using a brake to check the force of the timber's descent. Others stood ready to catch planks as they plummeted down the chute. "As each man gets a piece of timber he runs with it, lays it down exactly where it belongs, and returns to the chute," Carl Rydell, an experienced schooner captain, reported. "It is difficult for a man below to catch a timber at the right instant and to get the right hold. If he makes a single slip, or if the brake is not applied in time, he may be injured or killed."

The wire loading method was a faster, safer way to load cargo. By the 1860s, a wharf had been built on the point west of Pigeon Point's beach, and a heavy cable strung to the peak of the inlet. Schooners, like the *Point Arena*, moored under this wire, and freight was brought aboard and sent ashore in slings.

Although this system was able to handle loads coming off the vessel as efficiently as loads going on board, it required considerable power ashore. It also made it more difficult for the vessel to get underway quickly in an emergency because the cable was often strung between the masts.

Apparently, at one point the cable was fastened to a giant rock in the bay, known as Monument Rock. "Out about 200 yards from shore is a high monument-like rock, rising to a level with the steep rock bluff which half encloses the bay," author and adventurer Colonel Albert S. Evans observed. "From the bluff to the top of this rock stretches a heavy wire cable, kept taut by a capstan."

"A vessel rounding the reef runs into the sheltered cove under this hawser, and then casts anchor. Slings running down on the hawser are rigged, and her cargo lifted from her deck load by load, run up into the air 50 to 100 feet, then hauled in shore, and landed upon the top of the bluff," Evans explained. "Lumber, hay, fruit, potatoes, vegetables, dairy products are in like manner run out upon the vessel's deck. If a

Passengers riding wire loading cable from the schooner Irene *to shore in a West Coast "dog hole" port.* G. Olsen Collection.

southwester comes on she slips her anchor and runs out to sea till it's over."

The business of cutting timber and of loading ships at Pigeon Point was taken over by the Beadle Steamship Company in 1910. They used a "high line" system, stretching a long cable from a post on the cliff to the mast of a vessel anchored off shore. Timber was conveyed in slings down the wire directly to the deck of the waiting schooner.

"It's Just Lumber"

Built in San Francisco in 1887 by Alexander Hay, the *Point Arena* made countless runs up and down the Pacific Coast delivering timber for the Beadle Steamship Company, plying the waters as far north as Vancouver Island, Canada and as far south as San Pedro, California. With a length of 115 feet, a beam of 31 feet, a depth of 9 feet, and measuring just over 200 tons, the little ship gave extraordinary service.

The *Point Arena* was one of 225 wooden steam schooners produced on the West Coast between 1885 and 1923. Two-masted ships with fore and aft sails, the vessels became popular because they steered easily in small harbors, required few crew, and were economical to maintain. "They are excellent sea boats," shipbuilder Henry Hull declared.

Steam schooners combined the proven seaworthiness of sailing schooners first built in the 1700s with the development of the marine steam engine. These versatile vessels were agile enough to maneuver well in small, hazardous coastal ports like Pigeon Point, yet sturdy enough to carry sizeable loads of cargo to larger ports. In essence, they were the trucks of their day.

Virtually all lumber and tanbark went by ship well after 1900. Enterprises such as the Beadle Steamship Company provided substantial sources of employment, as well as important building and leather-making materials, encouraged settlement of areas ignored by miners and farmers, and drew money into local communities. In a single year, over 5,000 tons of tanbark alone could be shipped from Pigeon Point to tanneries throughout the San Francisco Bay area.

A.W. Beadle, managing partner of the firm bearing his name, zealously sought commissions and charters. He kept schooners like the *Point Arena*, and their masters, under perpetual pressure to transport heavier payloads. "The captain will have to load the vessel deeper if we

Built in 1887 as a coastal schooner, the Point Arena *made countless runs up and down the Pacific Coast delivering lumber and other cargo.* San Francisco Maritime National Historical Park.

are going to make any money with her," the irascible Beadle complained. "She will carry a big load if he will only put it on."

The *Point Arena* was specially suited for her role in the Pacific coastal trade. A broad beamed, single deck ship, she carried prodigious loads in her hold and on deck. Old-timers claimed that these loads were piled on until the deck itself was sometimes under four feet of water.

"I see Beadle work for Beadle," James T. Smith, one of A.W. Beadle's schooner captains huffed. To his and other protests over the vast quantity of timber cast aboard the little vessels, Beadle's crusty reply is said to have been, "Hell, it's just lumber. You've never seen wood sink have you?"

Worn and Weary Schooner

On her final call to Pigeon Point, the *Point Arena's* captain, John Halvorsen, took the routine precautions. The captain knew the inlet offered scant protection from unforeseen storms or treacherous currents. He knew an abrupt swell or a sudden lull or shift in the wind could spell disaster. Those dangers were just part of the job.

The steamer had survived two previous mishaps. In 1904, she went aground at Point Reyes, about forty miles north of San Francisco, and later, ran ashore farther north along the lumber coast. Bottom up, she was towed each time to safety into San Francisco and repaired.

In the early morning hours of August 9, 1913, despite strong southeast winds and choppy seas, the *Point Arena* began loading her usual cargo of tanbark manifested for San Francisco. Unexpectedly, the schooner fouled a mooring line in her propeller. Although Capt. Halvorsen "tried to maneuver the vessel out" to deeper water, the wind caught her stern. The defenseless ship lurched violently, slamming broadside into the rocks. Lifting and falling with the breakers, she tore a hole amidships.

As the sea foamed over the deck, the captain ordered his eighteen-man crew to abandon ship. The stunned seamen could only watch the *Point Arena* sink into the churning water. A surge of surf lifted her into the air and dropped her back down, impaling the worn schooner on the rocks. Mercilessly, heavy waves crashed through the stricken vessel, sending a geyser of seawater high above the mast. Held captive by the rocks, the *Point Arena's* end was near.

The Point Arena *after she wrecked while loading cargo in 1913.* Frank Perry/Frank Davis.

The broken ship, valued at $25,000, was burned as a potential hazard to navigation. "It just would not have looked good," local resident Frank Davis exclaimed, "to have a wrecked ship in front of a lighthouse."

Testimony to the Past

Although the Beadle Steamship Company prospered into the late 1930s, shipping at Pigeon Point waned after World War I. Largely, it became less expensive to haul freight by truck. The mid-1920s saw the end of "loading under wire," and of Pigeon Point as a port.

A section of the *Point Arena*'s starboard bow washed into the mouth of Greenoaks Creek near Año Nuevo, where it lay buried by sand for nearly seventy years. Fierce storms on the coast in 1983 exposed the five-ton fragment. The jagged remnant still bears an iron cleat and, above and below two portholes, the ship's name. Standing as testimony to the past, it is on display at Año Nuevo State Reserve.

Monument Rock still stands, too. The stony sculpture protruding off Pigeon Point's shore is not just an ordinary rock. Along with others in the bay, it is part of the California Coastal National Monument. These unique pinnacles are protected biological sites that provide shelter and nutrients for seabirds, pinnipeds, plant life, and thousands of other marine organisms.

The *Point Arena*'s ashes long ago settled amidst the surrounding waters. After years of service, the Pacific workhorse is at rest.

A five-ton fragment of the Point Arena*'s burned hull, washed ashore in 1983, is on display at Año Nuevo State Reserve.* Author's Collection.

7

DECKS AWASH

MAY 22, 1925

Smuggling liquor, the schooner *Pilgrim,* one of a flotilla of elusive rum runners, ran afoul of the rocks beneath Pigeon Point Lighthouse.

Rum Row

Throughout the 1920s, when Prohibition was in full swing, the flow of liquor from the sea was unprecedented. Joseph C. Allen's "The Smugglers' Chanty," captures the essence of the times: "Tis easy and free for us boys out at sea, way-o, whiskey and gin! Pigs will all fly when the country goes dry. Give us the word and we'll run the rum in."

The practice of smuggling liquor is as old as the substance itself. In the 1500s, the British government operated revenue cutters to stop smugglers. Pirates created lucrative enterprises running rum to heavily taxed colonies. As early as 1600, nautical terms appeared to describe a state of inebriation, including "three sheets to the wind," "listing to starboard," "carrying too much sail," and "decks awash."

By far the most famous period of rum running occurred in the United States between 1920 and 1933. The passing of the 18th Amendment, also known as the Volstead Act, on October 28, 1919, prohibited the sale, possession, and consumption of alcohol. It proved to be an extremely unpopular law. Reveling in an otherwise liberated era, many citizens enjoyed a good stiff drink now and again, even if it was illegal.

The first few months of Prohibition were deceptively quiet along America's shores. One of the earliest official references to the growing illicit trade was in the Coast Guard's 1921 annual report. The Florida coast patrol was cited as "particularly vigilant, having made hundreds of trips to support Prohibition authorities and seize vessels."

A Florida boat builder and excursion boat captain named Bill McCoy, who became the self-styled "King of the Rum Runners," set the pattern for smuggling liquor by sea. He brought ships to the edge of the three-mile limit of U.S. jurisdiction and sold his wares to "contact boats" owned by local fishermen and small boat captains. McCoy was famous for never watering his booze, and selling only top-of-the-line name brands. Reputedly, this was the origin of the term "The Real McCoy," meaning genuine and on the level.

As the demand for illegal liquor grew, so did the enticements of rum running. Soon, the idea caught on with hundreds of other boat owners along the country's coastlines. For many, it was the only way to make a living. "I was in the rum running business for a couple of years," one skipper admitted. "It was the only dollar you could make."

The three-mile limit became known as the "Rum Line," and vessels waiting to receive illegal spirits were called "Rum Row." In 1924, the Rum Line was extended to a twelve-mile limit, making it more difficult for smaller and less seaworthy craft to travel the distance. With the run to shore longer, chances of detection increased. In a desperate attempt to avoid arrest, some rum runners dumped their cargo, set the vessel on fire, and abandoned ship.

Often, crews armed themselves against government ships and against other rum runners. Some rum boats sank others to hijack precious cargo, rather than journey to Canada or Mexico to restock their liquid supplies. At night, even in fog, they often ran at high speeds and without lights. Many smashed into rocks, spilling their profits overboard.

Ironically, one thing that rum runners seldom carried was rum. The name was a holdover from the rum smuggling of colonial days, and from the habit of referring to all liquor as the "demon rum." Most of the cargo was whiskey bottled in Canada and Mexico by professional distillers.

A rum-running ship, similar to the Pilgrim, *with her deck filled with cases and barrels of illegal whiskey and beer.* U.S. Coast Guard.

After California voted to join other dry states, rum runners flocked to the coast. Secluded coves like Pigeon Point were ideal locations for their illegal operations. Newspapers of the era are filled with accounts of coastside prohibition squads searching for huge caches of smuggled liquor. On one occasion, "Agents received word of four motor boats that made several trips from Rum Row to the coast off Pigeon Point and landed a cargo of 2,000 cases of whiskey."

Carrie Nation's Navy

The task of pursuing rum runners was assigned to the U.S. Coast Guard, a small arm of the Treasury Department. When Prohibition began in 1920, the service was ill-equipped to cope with zealous lawbreakers. Thousands of miles of coast had to be patrolled by a fleet of fewer than 100 ships and a meager workforce of 4,000. Some reports indicate that no more than five percent of the U.S. bound liquor was stopped between 1920 and 1925.

Nicknamed "Carrie Nation's Navy" after the hatchet-swinging temperance leader, Coast Guard vessels consisted of an assortment of cruising cutters, inshore patrol boats, and harbor cutters. As the rum tide continued to rise in epidemic proportions, pressure built to develop a fleet designed to meet the growing problem. "The Coast Guard's force could prevent only a small part of the illegal traffic," Commandant William E. Reynolds said, "one entirely unprecedented in the history of the country."

During 1925, Coast Guard personnel increased to over 10,000. The largest single element of the expansion was the construction of 203 new patrol boats. Twenty-five of the ships were built on the West Coast. These sturdy 75-foot vessels, known as "six-bitters," became the mainstay of the Rum War. The nickname came from the colloquial term of "six bits," meaning 75 cents. Placing the vessels in service accounted for fifty percent of the authorized personnel increases.

Designed for 17 knots and a crew of eight, the new patrol boats emphasized seaworthiness and endurance over speed. Intended for offshore work, the vessels picketed rum ships beyond the twelve-mile limit to prevent contact boats from obtaining their loads of liquor. They were armed with machine guns and a one-pound rapid fire gun. Aiding a more aggressive stance toward rum runners were new agreements with other maritime nations which allowed the Coast Guard to patrol twenty to thirty miles at sea.

A Coast Guard patrol boat, known as a "six-bitter," tows a captured rum runner into San Francisco. U.S. Coast Guard.

Among the boats used by the Coast Guard to chase down rum runners were those built as sub-chasers and converted to Prohibition duty. Shown is the Electra, *which later became Franklin D. Roosevelt's presidential yacht, USS* Potomac. National Archives.

Sometimes, information received during the capture of one rum running ship led to hooking a bigger fish. "Wallowing in heavy seas south of Pigeon Point, a Coast Guard vessel captured a power boat and towed it to San Francisco with 350 cases of imported whiskey and two prisoners aboard," a local newspaper reported. "Based on information provided by the smugglers, the Coast Guard intensified patrols searching for another rum runner believed to be carrying a cargo of 20,000 cases of whiskey."

Quite Ruthless Men

Waterborne smugglers flocked to Pigeon Point's secluded coves. With its many landing spots, proximity of good roads, and relatively sparse population, the area was a perfect place for their clandestine operations.

In the pre-dawn hours of May 22, 1925, the *Pilgrim* came to grief on the rocks near Pigeon Point. Aboard was a cargo of illegal brew valued at $10,000. Much to the chagrin of many thirsty souls, Coast Guard patrol boats reached the scene quickly and confiscated the spirits after the *Pilgrim* drifted from the rocks to a sand bar. Not a single drop of the contraband, consisting of 175 cases of whiskey and 100 barrels of beer, sloshed overboard.

The *Pilgrim's* flustered two-man crew scattered hastily, having already transferred much of the cache to waiting automobiles. According to Coast Guard officials, the racketeers nearly drowned attempting to salvage the remaining goods.

Owned by Enoch Olson of Astoria, Oregon, the *Pilgrim* was operated "by a young scion of a prominent bay area family who was in the game for adventure." Rum running held an allure for others, too. "If drinking the stuff is half as much fun as running it," one smuggler declared, "I can understand the drinker's problem."

In this instance, local residents were left high and dry. The following day, prohibition agents located a hidden store of spirits believed to be part of the *Pilgrim's* cargo. "There was a truckload of whiskey," officials in Half Moon Bay exclaimed.

With a length of 75 feet and measuring 15 tons, the *Pilgrim* was larger than other rum boats. Generally, the vessels were inexpensive to build, and were designed for relatively short hauls at high speed. Known as the "mosquito fleet," the vessels were small, astonishingly fast, and adept at quick shoreline "sting operations." Most were 30 to 40 feet long, with virtually bare hulls, and small engines. Surplus wartime water-cooled aircraft engines turning out 200 to 300 horsepower were easily found and adapted. Some carried machine guns, even armor plating. Many kept cans of used oil handy to pour on hot exhaust manifolds, in case a smoke screen was needed to escape patrol boats.

The *Pilgrim* was not alone in finding Pigeon Point's isolated beaches a perfect setting for illicit activity. One night, Assistant Keeper Jesse Mygrants interrupted a band of rum runners. At gunpoint, he was forced to drive them eight miles down the coast to their next destination.

"They were quite ruthless men," his daughter, Jessie Mygrants Davis, declared. "We'd watch for them. They always came on moonlit nights, so we could see them clearly. They sailed in on the south side of the tower and were audacious enough to use the lighthouse derrick to unload their ships. Once, one of the dories hit the rocks and the cargo was lost. There were lots of divers in the area after that."

Many local residents were engaged in the liquor traffic. Upon returning from a dance, Jessie and her sister encountered smugglers who recognized their car. Apparently, their dates for the evening were acquainted with the smugglers. "They told us to go straight into the house," she recalled. "We were scared and shaking, and got ready for bed with the lights out. Then, all we could hear was the squeak of the derrick winch."

Drink Hearty

Towed twenty-five miles north to Half Moon Bay, the *Pilgrim* was sold later to San Francisco's Western Fishing Company where she served as a fishing schooner. Her rum running days were over. However, it was not uncommon for an impounded rum boat to be sold for a paltry sum at auction, often back to the original owner. Vessels brazenly reappeared, frequently under different names, made their habitual rounds, and were captured several times.

Prohibition, along with rum running, ended in 1933. Between 1925 and the close of Prohibition, the Coast Guard seized nearly 500 rum ships. Most were burned or destroyed as unsafe and unfit for use. Contact boats still in the hands of small boat owners were sold or scrapped. Many crew members sought service in the merchant marine or the U.S. Navy. Welcomed as skilled and experienced seamen, former rum runners often joined non-commissioned officer ranks.

Assistant Keeper Jesse Mygrants caught rum runners unloading their cargo under Pigeon Point's tower. Frank Perry/Frank Davis.

The U.S. Coast Guard emerged from Prohibition a more efficient service. "The fight against liquor smuggling is one of the most complex naval operations ever executed," Rear Admiral Frederick C. Billard asserted. "The Coast Guard was given the task and it did not discuss it or argue about it. It simply answered, 'Aye, Aye, Sir,' and sailed into the job."

The organization grew substantially in ships, personnel, and experience. New skills, such as the ability to conduct effective intelligence operations, developed from battling rum runners. During World War II, those skills were essential when the Coast Guard was called to defend America's shores.

In all likelihood, the once forbidden cocktail will never be as tantalizing as it was in the 1920s. Even so, the colorful refrain of Joseph C. Allen's "Song of the Rumrunner" lingers on. "Fill up again with the red, red rum. Drink hearty, my lads, and deep."

8

A Tragic Voyage

August 29, 1929

Pigeon Point's worst maritime disaster occurred on August 29, 1929, when the passenger steamer *San Juan* collided with an oil tanker twice her size. Lost in the wreck was an historic ship, a captain's reputation, and many promising and productive lives.

Pacific Mail Fleet

Built by John Roach and Sons in 1882, the *San Juan* took her first dip into the water at Chester, Pennsylvania. The iron-hulled steamer's maiden voyage was as part of the Pacific Mail Steamship Company's fleet. Although later sister ships such as the *Colombia* were larger, at 2,076 gross tons, a length of 283 feet and a beam of 37 feet, the *San Juan* was one of the finest the company owned.

The *San Juan* was part of a long line of ships born out of the 1840s, a decade that witnessed the successful application of steam to the operation of oceangoing vessels. With the California gold rush, steamers proved their worth, demonstrating their practicality for long voyages with greater speed and regularity than sailing vessels. The Pacific Mail Steamship Company was chartered during this period, offering the quickest travel and communication alternative to those eager for adventure in and information about "the new El Dorado of the West."

The Isthmus of Panama became an important route between the eastern United States and California. Many prospectors sailed from Atlantic ports, crossed the Isthmus by wagon, on mules, and on foot, and then took another ship for California. The Panama route shortened the voyage between New York and San Francisco to less than 6,000 miles. Previously, ships making the trip traveled around Cape Horn, a distance of nearly 15,000 miles.

Over time, the steamers employed on the Panama route changed little. The distinctive deckhouse extended from one end of the vessel to the other, and contained passenger staterooms and officers' quarters. A hurricane deck formed a canopy over the entire length and breadth of the ship. This design greatly increased deck space for passengers and was particularly welcome on vessels operating in tropical waters.

The late 1860s were characterized by great expansion of the Pacific Mail fleet. During the Civil War, the importance of the service it rendered was significant, forming as it did the chief means of communication between the eastern and western areas of the embattled Union. Passenger travel west was heavy, and after the Civil War, an increased amount of freight was sent by way of Panama. The fleet enjoyed a reputation as "The most universally popular steamship line in the world." Competing lines were described by the press as "floating pig stys."

Through the 1880s and 1890s, Pacific Mail began offering trans-Pacific services while continuing to strengthen its coastal operations. A dozen vessels, including the *San Juan*, were built and purchased for the San Francisco to Panama route. In 1920, Pacific Mail attained its greatest size, with forty-six steamers operating under its house flag.

The *San Juan*, and the rest of Pacific Mail's coastal fleet, was sold to W.R. Grace and Company in June of 1925. By that time, Grace held controlling interest in the successful enterprise. He sold the house flag, good will, and trade name of Pacific Mail to the Dollar Steamship Company, a popular world-wide shipping line, the following year.

After sailing the seas for more than forty years, the *San Juan* was towed to the Oakland mudflats. The stalwart steamer lay there with rusting plates and peeling paint until purchased at auction by the Los Angeles-San Francisco Navigation Company's "White Flyer" Line. She was put back into service in 1927. Unfortunately, the *San Juan* met her end a mere two years later.

Pigeon Point's worst maritime disaster occurred when the passenger steamer San Juan *collided with an oil tanker.* San Mateo County History Museum.

Capt. Adolf F. Asplund was dubbed a "hoodoo" skipper because of his jinxed history. San Jose Mercury News.

"Hoodoo" Skipper

During her final voyage, the *San Juan* carried seventy-three passengers and forty-four crew. The steamer, the oldest ship in regular passenger service on the Pacific Coast, promised a delightful way to travel. The journey was marketed as, "The economical way that entails no sacrifice. One fare includes comfortable berth, excellent meals, open-air dancing, promenade decks, radio music. All the luxury of ocean travel."

Filling in for the regular master of the ship was Capt. Adolf F. Asplund. Dubbed a "hoodoo" skipper because of his jinxed history, Asplund struggled to keep a good reputation afloat. On one occasion his license was suspended for allowing his vessel to sail without a full complement in the engine department. After a collision with a launch in Oakland Creek caused one death, his license was suspended again. Later, upon running a steam schooner aground, he lost his ticket for a year.

Asplund continued to be haunted by ill luck. Just before midnight on August 29, 1929, the *San Juan* and the *S.C.T. Dodd*, a 4,374-ton Standard Oil tanker, sighted each other just three-quarters of a mile apart. The *San Juan*, traveling at 11.3 knots in fog-obscured waters, saw the tanker on the port bow and tried to change course to starboard. The *S.C.T. Dodd*, making 10.5 knots, saw the steamer on the starboard bow and attempted to go full speed astern.

The tanker struck the *San Juan* near the engine room about seventy-five feet from her stern. The *San Juan*'s lights went out at the moment of collision. Within five minutes, she sank stern first. Survivors exclaimed, "The *San Juan* smashed like kindling wood." The *S.C.T. Dodd*, still afloat, showed effects of the crushing impact, sustaining eight-inch gashes on either side of the bow just above the waterline. The stem of the steel vessel was twisted severely by the shock of the crash.

Most of the *San Juan*'s passengers were trapped while asleep below deck. "I was in my stateroom when a shattering impact awakened me. The ship shivered violently, and a wave of green water swept in," survivor Margie Dansby relayed. "Getting on deck, I was swept overboard by the next wave. The water was rough, and the fog was so thick I couldn't see."

Others were less fortunate. Men, women, and children from all walks of life sank with the steamer, including Mrs. Willie Jasmine Brown.

Officers of the passenger steamer San Juan. San Francisco Maritime National Historical Park.

Mrs. Willie Jasmine Brown, a passenger who perished aboard the San Juan, *took the ship because it was cheaper than the train.* Author's Collection/Lorraine Spinelli.

Also lost was George Navarro, a teenage movie extra. National Archives and Records Administration.

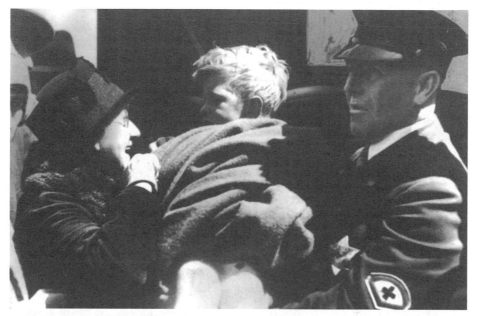

Hollis Lee Pifer, the only child to survive the wreck, was saved when his mother threw him onto the deck of the S.C.T. Dodd. San Francisco Maritime National Historical Park.

Her last letter declared, "I'd really rather take the train, but the boat is cheaper. The children need shoes." The fare from San Francisco to San Pedro, California was, indeed, attractively priced. The cost for sailing between the ports was $8 to $10 per person.

Also lost was: George Navarro, a teenage movie extra, who appeared in films featuring Ronald Coleman and Victor McLaglen; and Marjorie Pifer, who saved her son, the only child to survive the wreck, by throwing him onto the deck of the *S.C.T. Dodd* as the *San Juan* disappeared beneath the sea. The accident took seventy-five lives, fifty-five passengers and twenty crew, more than any other shipwreck in the area's history.

Running at Full Speed

A sensational scandal followed the collision. To charges that the *San Juan* was unseaworthy, officials responded, "The *Titanic*, a new ship, sank almost immediately when she received a blow comparable to that received by the *San Juan*."

Given that the *San Juan* carried lifesaving equipment of six lifeboats and 127 life preservers, speculation ran rampant as to why so few passengers were saved. Newspaper headlines of the time screamed "Cowardly Desertion of Passengers." One account charged, "When the crash came, the entire crew deserted their posts to save themselves and made no effort to launch a boat or save a soul."

Others charged the *S.C.T. Dodd*, which was badly gashed but managed to stay afloat, with pulling away from the *San Juan* too soon. They maintained that the tanker could have saved more lives by staying with the wreckage. More likely, it was the speed with which the *San Juan* went down. "We heard the crash and the lights went out," the *San Juan*'s Second Officer recalled. "Then, in a second I got covered with water and the vessel sank from under me."

Officers and crew of each vessel blamed the other for changing course and causing the accident. According to the *San Juan*'s Third Officer Robert Papenfuss, "The *Dodd* changed course and was headed directly for us." The Quartermaster added, "If the *Dodd* had continued on course when we first saw her, she would have gone clear of the ship."

Officers of the *S.C.T. Dodd* saw the events differently. Third Officer Otto V. Saunders reported, "All of a sudden the other vessel changed course." Capt. Hugo O. Bleumchen insisted, "If the *San Juan* had continued going full ahead when I signaled that I was going full speed astern, this collision would have been avoided."

The controversy continued during a trial charging Capt. Bleumchen with inattention to duty, and Officers Saunders and Papenfuss with unskillfullness. Having left explicit instructions in the night order book governing the actions of the bridge officers, Bleumchen emerged unscathed. He continued his career and died in 1953 at the age of seventy-one.

Hard luck followed Capt. Asplund to the end. Although he went down with the *San Juan*, along with all of her logs and records, the court held him at fault for "running his vessel at full speed in the fog, and failing to maintain a proper lookout."

However, responsibility was also placed on both Third Officers: Papenfuss, for not calling Capt. Asplund at once when he sighted the tanker, and Saunders, for not following instructions and for not reducing speed on the *S.C.T. Dodd* before entering the fog bank. Their licenses were suspended for a year.

Families and relatives of those aboard the *San Juan* flooded the District Court with lawsuits. In January of 1932, the final decree fixing claimants' damages was settled. Standard Oil paid a total of just over $329,000 in death, personal injury, lost effects, and lost cargo claims. Of that, awards for deaths amounted to about $144,000, or approximately $1,900 per person lost.

The *S.C.T. Dodd* was repaired and continued to sail. In 1943 the War Shipping Administration took possession of the tanker and delivered it to the Soviet Union for wartime service.

Not all of the *San Juan* remained on the ocean floor. The deckhouse floated to the surface on November 14, 1929, bearing sad witness to a tragic voyage.

9

SARDINES
AND SORROWS

FEBRUARY 2, 1932
SEPTEMBER 18, 1934

Seized by inclement weather, the *Western Spirit* and the *Ohio No. 3* crashed into the rocks just yards from Pigeon Point Lighthouse. The wrecks left no doubt that sardine fishing is a hazardous occupation. Regrettably, fishing proved equally hazardous for the sardines.

The "Wetfish" Fleet

The waters off Pigeon Point were, and still are, popular fishing grounds. Appropriately, the community surrounding Pigeon Point, called Pescadero, means "fishing place" in Spanish. Named for its bountiful inland trout streams, the area is known also for its vast offshore harvest of salmon and sardines.

Traditionally, sardines, also called pilchard, were canned "wet from the sea" with little pre-processing. Because of this, they were dubbed "wetfish." Sardine fishermen, hauling their catch aboard using huge purse seine nets, were drenched in a shower of seawater, giving the term a double meaning. The work was both soggy and cumbersome.

Purse seiners, like the *Western Spirit* and the *Ohio No. 3*, caught sardines near the ocean surface by encircling them with a long net.

*Sardine fishermen, hauling their catch aboard using large nets, were drenched in a
shower of fish and saltwater.* Maritime Museum of Monterey.

They all operated on the same principle: surrounding and trapping fish by closing the bottom of the net, much like the drawstrings on an old-fashioned purse. Although the purse seine net was more efficient than earlier nets, it was also heavier and harder to maneuver.

Purse seiners first cruised into Monterey Bay in 1926. The vessels were wider, deeper, and heavier than existing boats called "Monterey Clippers." Additionally, they were designed to carry most of the load in the hold rather than on deck. Within a decade, seiners proved better adapted to large-scale fishing.

The vessels incorporated a protected wheel-house and cabin, large diesel engines, power winches for the giant purse seine net, a revolving turntable aft on which the net was stacked for deployment, and a large hold capacity. As a result, greater amounts of sardines, each routinely reaching 11 to 14 inches in length, could be snared. Monterey Clippers, which were too small to carry crew, net, and fish, towed a barge or "lighter" in which to load the catch for transport back to the pier.

Sardines were off-loaded into buckets 500 pounds at a time, and hoisted by cable to the canneries. The pilchard was measured and weighed, then sent to cutting sheds. In the early 1930s, the bucket and cable method was replaced by a system of floating wooden pens, or "hoppers," anchored safely out from Monterey Bay's dangerous reefs. Hoppers were connected to the canneries by large pipe-like underwater hoses, employing massive pumps to literally suck the sardines ashore for processing.

"The sardine is ubiquitous, and such a modest fish," William Ellis Ripley mused in Ode to the Sardine of Monterey Bay, "But when it's on the table, it's such a tasty dish."

Cannery Row

Originally, the grueling work of preparing and packing sardine tins along Monterey's "Cannery Row" was almost exclusively done by women. Often before dawn, a chorus of cannery whistles, each with its own pitch and pattern, called workers to the lines and warehouses. Cutting, packing, and cooking continued until that night's catch was canned, no matter how long it took.

Sardines were cut by hand, drained, and dried on wooden slats or "flakes." Large flat metal baskets of flaked fish were drawn through long troughs of boiling peanut oil, drained again, packed into cans, and hand soldered closed. Labeling and boxing for warehousing and shipment completed the operation. These canning processes prevailed until World War I when canneries were mechanized.

During the war, the sardine industry surged. Orders for non-perishable canned fish poured in from both civilian and military buyers. Cannery Row's wartime sardine production grew from 75,000 cases in 1915 to 1.4 million cases in 1918. Similarly, the price per case rose from $2.14 to $7.50. Eventually, Cannery Row housed over twenty sardine processing plants.

At a time when certain proof could not be produced to the contrary, cannery owner Knute Hovden remarked smugly, "The sardine supply cannot be exterminated."

The wartime bonanza was, of course, too good to last. The end of World War I, and its ensuing recession, saw a scramble for survival by the sardine factories along Cannery Row. Reduction of sardines into fertilizer and fish meal, once a profitable sideline to canning, became a separate and dominant industry.

The Great Depression of the 1930s was softened for the local area by the general success of Monterey's sardine industry. As the sardine fleet and the canning capacity expanded, an average catch of over 100,000 tons per season was recorded through the decade. The industry reached its peak in 1934, yielding over 230,000 tons of sardines.

The trend continued during World War II, with the catch averaging over 200,000 tons per season. Pacific sardines accounted for one fourth of all the fish landed in the United States. Monterey became "The Sardine Capital of the World."

Silver Tide

Counted among Monterey's renowned sardine fleet, the *Western Spirit* and the *Ohio No. 3* often traveled northward from Monterey, fishing off Santa Cruz, Año Nuevo Point, and Pigeon Point. The vessels caught sardines at night, when the turbulence of the fishes' acre-sized schools, or shoals, caused the ocean surface to glow. Once spotted, the seiners cast their nets deep into the silver tide.

"The boat circles the gleaming shoal and drifts out her seine net. They close the circle and purse the bottom of the net, then with great labor haul it in," poet Robinson Jeffers wrote. "I cannot tell you how beautiful the scene is, and a little terrible, when the crowded fish know they are caught."

The Western Spirit, *a purse seiner, was part of Monterey's well-known sardine fleet.* Los Angeles Maritime Museum.

Before she wrecked, the Ohio No. 3 *often returned to shore with a deck load of fish.* Maritime Museum of Monterey.

Finding shoals of fish at night requires far more than fisherman's luck. On moonless nights, it took experience and skill to spot the "green flash" of schooling sardines. And the arduous task of deploying an unwieldy net off a moving boat on the open sea in total darkness took teamwork and courage.

The process of catching the fish, or "making a set," begins by dropping a skiff containing one end of the net off the back of the seiner. Crewmen in the skiff deploy a sea anchor, a parachute-like device that when submerged acts like a brake, allowing the purse seiner to pull away and arc through the sardines.

The seiner completes encirclement of the catch and connects its end of the net to the skiff. A cable running through rings at the bottom of the lead-weighted net is drawn in by power-winch to purse the net below the fish. A boom and tackle lift the net to a turntable as the winch draws in the pursed net until the last section of the net, the bag, draws alongside the seiner.

Fish are transferred from bag to boat by a large dip-net, resembling a horn-of-plenty when tipped, and emptied into the seiner's hold. If the bag contained more sardines than the capacity of the hold, it was common to pour the excess pilchard onto the vessel's walkways and deck.

Happy with her large catch, the boat waddled back to shore with a "deck load" of fish. At port, author John Steinbeck noted, "Silver rivers of fish poured out of the boats."

Harrowing Experience

Fishing boats frequently braved unfavorable weather searching for sardines. On February 2, 1932, as light rain and steady winds followed the *Western Spirit* from Monterey, the captain and crew thought little of it. Built by the Western Boat Building Company of Tacoma, Washington around 1926, the *Western Spirit* had weathered her share of rough seas.

However, shortly after midnight, the worst storm in twenty years lashed the seiner with sleet, hail, and a terrific downpour of rain. Winds increased to gale force. Blinded by the squall and trying desperately to locate Pigeon Point's beam of light, the vessel crashed broadside into the rocks just off shore.

Mountainous waves lifted the helpless ship high into the air and banged it back down on the rocks, crushing the only lifeboat. Relentless breakers tumbled the helpless craft to within 100 yards of shore. With the

Bound for the fishing grounds, the Western Spirit *crashed into the rocks just yards from Pigeon Point Lighthouse.* Frank Perry/Jesse Mygrants Davis.

Pigeon Point Lighthouse's Head Keeper Gerhard W. Jaehne saved the crew of the Western Spirit. Author's Collection/Claude and Jenny Bond.

crew clinging frantically to the deck to avoid being washed overboard, Capt. Tony Oreb sounded incessant whistle blasts as a distress signal.

Ashore, Head Keeper Gerhard W. Jaehne heard the signals and saw the vessel's bobbing lights. Rushing to the rescue, he threw a line aboard. Capt. Oreb struggled through the swirling surf to shore, dragging a heavier line from the *Western Spirit*. Guided only by a hand lantern and the flashing beam of the lighthouse, the two men continued working the lines, pulling ten bedraggled crewmen to safety.

"Eleven haggard and exhausted men stood in the pouring rain at 5:00 A.M. and solemnly shook hands with Keeper Jaehne," a local newspaper reported. "They had just escaped a harrowing experience that goes down in coast marine history as an epic of the fishing industry."

After receiving First Aid, the captain and crew were taken in a truck to San Francisco. Betraying the terrible pounding she had endured from the storm, the *Western Spirit* lay beneath the lighthouse tower, battered and abandoned.

Foundered in Fog

Another Monterey purse seiner, the *Ohio No. 3* was built in 1929 by Anderson and Christofani of San Francisco. "They had a thing about craftsmanship," one company shipwright boasted. "This was a real bone in the ship yard." She was 72 feet long, 20 feet wide, and carried 100 tons of fish when fully loaded.

No doubt, the *Ohio No. 3* was a fine, sturdy vessel. She was also the first Japanese owned purse seiner in Monterey. The cost of entry into a competitive age of big boats and huge nets was astronomical by Monterey standards. The seiner cost $28,000 to build, and fishing equipment was equally expensive. Sardine nets alone ran $12,000 each.

The vessel's owner and captain was twenty-three year old Frank Manaka. "In those days, people were working for 25 to 50 cents an hour," he recalled. "We thought this was quite an investment."

Four years later, on September 18, 1934, Manaka nearly lost his investment, and his crew, when the *Ohio No. 3* ran up on the rocks 200 yards north of Pigeon Point. "We were bound for fishing ground," the captain reported, "when the ship foundered in fog and darkness."

Seaman S. Nojima risked his life to save the seiner and its twelve crew. When a line, taken ashore by a skiff, parted, Nojima dove into frigid water, fought the breakers, and swam to shore with a new line.

Capt. Frank Manaka reported that the Ohio No. 3 *foundered in fog and darkness.*
Maritime Museum of Monterey.

"Except for the new line," Manaka declared, "We would have been washed into deep water and sunk."

Two days later, with the help of a derrick, the *Ohio No. 3* was floated on fifty large steel drums, and lashed to a barge. As she was towed to San Francisco for repairs, only her bow showed above the water. Also salvaged was her valuable purse seine net, virtually undamaged.

A Fish Out of Water

Sadly, although other purse seiners would ply the waters off Pigeon Point, the *Western Spirit* would not. Owned by Capt. Oreb and the California Packing Corporation, now Del Monte, the $30,000 vessel was a total loss.

Left stranded on the beach, the *Western Spirit* broke apart and floated out to sea. According to Allen Petrich, grandson of the Western Boat Building Company's founder, Martin Petrich, the seiner "had put a lot of fish on the table."

Although he persevered, Capt. Manaka could not keep the *Ohio No. 3* afloat. "The cannery would allow the boats to go only once a week," he said, "which was not enough to keep up expenses." Sold to a San Pedro fisherman in 1937, the vessel continued to fish, but not for sardines. She sailed from Santa Cruz to the Mexican border catching tuna for the Van Camp Sea Food Cannery.

The sardine industry had been buoyed during depression and war by grinding pilchards into pulp, but the consequences were disastrous. Sardines, on the verge of extinction, began to disappear. "The answer to the question, 'where are all the sardines?' is obvious," marine biologist Edward F. "Doc" Ricketts exclaimed. "They're in the cans."

By the early 1950s the average annual catch dropped to under 20,000 tons. With no immediate usefulness for a fish-canning industry without fish, Cannery Row, later restored as a major tourist center, became a ghost town of empty warehouses and canneries. "Most of the sardines had been netted," Monterey resident Ed Larsh lamented, "and the entire industry was gasping like a fish out of water."

Shipwrecks remained an occupational hazard for Capt. Oreb and Capt. Manaka. In spite of grounding another vessel, Capt. Oreb stayed on to skipper fishing boats for the California Packing Corporation.

Eventually, Capt. Manaka returned to fishing. Partnering with the Western Boat Building Company, he skippered the *Western Spirit's* sister ship, the *Western Explorer*. Unfortunately, he lost the 150-ton tuna boat off Socorro Island, Mexico in 1956. Five crew, including Manaka's brother-in-law, drowned. Eight years later, another tuna boat sprang a leak and sank off the coast of Ecuador. Manaka sighed, "That was the last of my fishing career."

A silver age of fishing had truly come to an end.

10

OCEAN-GOING
BOXCAR

MARCH 17, 1953

Perhaps the most unusual vessel to wreck near Pigeon Point's shores was the *BARC 1*. Under tow by a large Army tug, the experimental barge amphibious resupply cargo craft disappeared mysteriously. Bobbing amid the breakers were the bodies of three crew, the only evidence of her untimely departure.

Swashbuckling Scientist

The *BARC 1* was designed by Dr. Thomas C. Poulter, a physicist and explorer who participated in the Second Byrd Antarctic Expedition in 1934. He is credited with saving Rear Admiral Richard E. Byrd's life, plowing his way in a snow tractor to the advance base hut where Byrd lay ill with carbon monoxide poisoning.

Following the expedition, Poulter became Associate Director of the Armour Research Foundation in Chicago, Illinois where he designed the Antarctic snow cruiser. A swashbuckler among scientists, Poulter capitalized on the excitement concerning Antarctic exploration by taking the vehicle on its first overland trip from Chicago to Boston and then to Philadelphia.

The BARC 1, *the first of four prototypes, was the only amphibious craft capable of landing on a beach through breaking surf.* U.S. Army Transport Museum.

Few events were more colorful. The machine was driven first to Grant Park in Chicago's Loop to demonstrate its maneuverability to the public before starting for Boston over the highways. As the vehicle lumbered across each state, the Highway Patrol stopped traffic all along the route. A special visit was made in New York so that blind children could "get a feel of the size of it."

In 1948 Poulter joined the Stanford Research Institute in Menlo Park, California, where he remained until his death at eighty-one in 1978. During that period, his research ranged widely, from the dynamic phenomena of explosives and ballistics to the communication of marine animals.

"I came to have an almost worshipful regard for Dr. Poulter's mechanical ingenuity, his intuitive use of physics and chemistry as a way of life," one of his students reminisced, "and his devotion to experimental research."

Boxcar Taking to Sea

When the Army Transportation Research and Development Station at Fort Eustis, Virginia inaugurated a feasibility study in August 1951 to create a large amphibious barge, Poulter was tapped to bring it to reality. The effort spawned a high capacity amphibious craft able to perform over-the-beach resupply missions far more efficiently than previously possible.

The *BARC 1* was one of the new concepts pioneered during the 1950s to inject greater efficiency into the Army transportation system. A critical problem was delivering cargo in harbors lacking pier facilities. At remote islands or isolated supply stations, goods were handled at least twice before reaching a final destination. In the urgency of war, these delays were a serious disadvantage. The *BARC 1* promised to be the solution.

The first of four prototypes, the *BARC 1* was built by the Pacific Car and Foundry Company of Seattle, Washington. In the 1950s, the firm was the leading builder of railway and industrial cars, including boxcars. The diversified enterprise also manufactured tractor winches, cranes, bulldozer equipment and fabricated steel for bridges, dams, and factories.

The *BARC's* dimensions were enough to dwarf any previous amphibian. The 100-ton barge was 61 feet long by 28 feet wide, with a height of nearly 20 feet. She carried 600 gallons of fuel and a crew of

Looking somewhat like a boxcar taking to sea, the BARC 1 *completed all preliminary tests.* U.S. Army Transport Museum.

The BARC's designer, Dr. Thomas C. Poulter, believed the craft was unsinkable. SRI International.

two to six men. The cargo compartment was spacious enough to carry huge vehicles, including a 34-ton Sherman tank and a 30-ton crane, in one load. Across the front was a ramp which could be lowered for loading or unloading motorized vehicles and other heavy equipment.

Propulsion in the water was accomplished by a pair of 48-inch diameter propellers. On land, each of the four wheels was independently driven by its own 165 horsepower diesel engine and an automatic three-speed transmission. The operating range with a normal sixty-ton payload was seventy-five miles in water, and 150 miles on land. In an emergency, an additional forty tons could be carried.

Another of the *BARC's* distinguishing features was her "crabbing" function. Both on land and on sea, she could move sideways in an indirect or diagonal manner. This meant the vessel had excellent maneuverability and could adeptly avoid obstacles strewn in her path.

The experimental *BARC 1* presented Poulter with a unique set of challenges. "I was given the job of testing it (for the Army Transportation Corps) for withstanding severe jolts that would be expected when coming in through heavy surf with a heavy load," he explained.

Initial tests were conducted at Fort Lawton, Washington in the Fall of 1952. The *BARC 1* was suspended on columns and jacked up to various heights. Then, the pins supporting the corners of the beams were filled with a small charge and exploded simultaneously. As the hefty craft plopped onto her tires, accelerometers calculated the force involved. Since the wheels were attached solidly to the body and lacked springs, it was essential that the tires were capable of absorbing the shock.

Other tests took place in the nearby waters of Puget Sound. "Looking somewhat like a boxcar taking to sea," one observer noted, the *BARC 1* paddled off and returned to shore in a slow arc. The world's largest amphibian crawled back upon the beach, climbed small dunes without lurching, then rolled smoothly up a sandy hillside with a 30-degree slope. Poulter declared proudly, "the *BARC 1* met all specifications."

"A Beast"

Developed to support a broad range of Army operations worldwide, the *BARC 1* was more than just a novelty. Over time, watercraft based on Poulter's prototype became essential in moving cargo from off-shore supply vessels to beaches or inland transfer areas.

In June 1954, one officer and twenty-seven enlisted men formed a Barge Amphibious Resupply Cargo Platoon to train in off-shore operations along the coast of Northern France. The exercises resulted from the fear that the Soviet Union, which had recently developed the nuclear bomb, might attack deep water ports difficult to supply.

One barge undertook its first mission in the Arctic in 1956, successfully carrying sixty tons of cargo from ship to shore. Four others were active in 1958 in Greenland delivering over 4,000 tons of cargo from supply ships to remote Army bases supporting the Distant Early Warning (DEW) Line. The DEW Line was a radar system built across Alaska, Canada, Newfoundland, Labrador, the Baffin Islands, and Greenland to protect the U.S. from Soviet attack.

During the Vietnam War, *BARCs* were used widely. Nearly every operation, whether on land or in water, was hazardous. Water operations were particularly dangerous due to adverse weather conditions and enemy action. These mighty amphibians were the only craft in the Army inventory capable of landing on a beach through breaking surf, carrying enormous loads of equipment and supplies.

"It was a beast, able to carry a medium sized locomotive," one veteran exclaimed. "It made an unforgettable sound."

Powerhouses though they were, the brawny barges had their disadvantages. On land the driver had no vision from the control cabin located near the rear of the craft, relying instead on hand signals from a crew member on the bow. On earlier hulls the control cabin was near the front, but raising and lowering of the loading ramp jarred the control panel badly.

The craft's greatest weakness was the air compressors. Located deep down in the engine room next to the marine gear, engineers often overlooked them in their engine checks. Since the entire system depended on air pressure, serious mishaps could occur.

In addition, the nine-foot tires tended to heat and swell to the bursting point, a common problem with amphibians. If one went flat, it took an hour to inflate. "Since the wheels on the *BARC* are larger," a crewman shrugged, "the problem is larger."

Although the exact number of *BARCs* built is unknown, at least fifty-four were once in operation. The last one was deactivated in 2001. In recent years, a few of the hardy barges have emerged for sale to the general public. Although, according to one salesman, "It's definitely a niche vehicle."

Difficult to Sink

The *BARC 1* raised much curiosity in the early 1950s. When she was shipped from Puget Sound, Washington to Monterey, California, inquisitive civilians took rides on the husky craft. "We cruised along at 10 to 15 miles per hour," reported one enthusiast. "It was like riding in a giant bathtub with wheels."

In her final evaluation tests, the *BARC 1* was side-launched into Monterey Bay from the deck of a tank landing ship. Confident of the seaworthiness of their craft, Capt. Marshall W. Esslinger and one crewman rode the amphibian down the twenty-three-foot drop.

It was a rocky finale. On the final plunge, the hulking barge was almost completely submerged by water. Nonetheless, the *BARC 1* took the dunking without mishap, and executed many successful beach landings buffeting waves as high as fifteen feet.

"It would be a difficult vessel to sink," Dr. Poulter insisted. One side of the barge's inner structure could be flooded, the ramp could be open, and a heavy load could weigh the craft down until the cargo deck was awash. Yet, the *BARC 1* could still make it to shore, climb the beach on the power of two engines, and roll to its destination at reduced speed.

When these tests were finished, the *BARC 1* was scheduled for towing to San Francisco. She was to sail under the Golden Gate Bridge on March 19, 1953 and proceed to the Presidio for a public demonstration. But the giant amphibian would face one last challenge. On February 23rd a howling sixty-mile-per-hour gale drove seven fishing vessels worth $500,000 from their moorings in Monterey Harbor.

Capt. Esslinger promptly agreed to use the *BARC 1* in the salvage efforts. He and his crew worked around the clock to salvage the stranded fishing boats. "The roar of its engines could be heard throughout Monterey," local newspapers reported, "as it churned through the sand pushing stranded boats like a bulldozer or pulled at them from deep water like a tug. It was a miracle."

Among those rescued was the $100,000 purse seiner, *Rosanna*. The 80-foot vessel was the last of the stranded ships to be floated. Unhappily, just three days later, the *Rosanna* sank off Pigeon Point while under tow to San Francisco for repairs. Apparently, her seams opened and she took on more water than the emergency pumps could handle.

"Criminal Stupidity"

On March 17, 1953, Capt. Esslinger insisted that the *BARC 1* depart at 1:30 P.M. rather than earlier which would have taken advantage of the

After a gale drove fishing boats ashore in Monterey, the BARC 1 *worked round the clock to rescue the stranded vessels.* Maritime Museum of Monterey.

maximum number of daylight hours. Unfortunately, as darkness, fog, and rough seas set in, trouble began.

In water, the *BARC's* maximum speed was 7.5 miles per hour. As the powerful Army tug towing her gained momentum, the *BARC 1* was swamped by heavy waves and pulled beneath the sea. The long stretch of cable and the fog prevented visual communication between the two ships, and for some baffling reason the *BARC 1* carried no radio.

In the murky darkness, the tug's captain saw nothing amiss until the cable parted. Although he contacted the Coast Guard to report the craft missing, it was too late. The *BARC 1* had disappeared, sinking in exactly the same spot as the *Rosanna*, the ship she had saved. Rescue units found Capt. Esslinger and two crew floating lifelessly amid the frigid waves, still clad in their lifejackets.

Local tugboat operators accused the Army of "criminal stupidity." Ultimately, the skippers of both vessels, and a series of errors, were blamed for sinking the experimental craft. "It began with the choice of an inexperienced tug captain. He never should have towed as fast as he did," Rear Admiral E.J. Moran stated. "Then, Capt. Esslinger fastened the towing bridles to the *BARC 1* near the waterline, where the crew could not release them in case of trouble."

In addition to the tug's excessive speed in rough seas, several mechanical failures aboard the *BARC 1* contributed to the disaster. These included a partial power failure, a fouled port pump, a clogged starboard drain, and a broken winch which prevented closing the vessel's ramp.

The tug boat captain was dismissed from his duties. Three months later, the *BARC 1* was raised from 220 feet of water, three miles off Pigeon Point. Buoyed to Oakland, where she was dismantled for investigation, the *BARC 1* finally completed her experimental journey.

Nevertheless, other units were built and used around the world. The *BARC 1* had proven her worth.

Once, lofty sailing ships, spunky schooners, and grand steamers traversed the legendary waters of Pigeon Point. The passage of the *BARC 1* signaled the end of an old era, and the beginning of a new one.

11

OTHER SHIPWRECKS

Two other known shipwrecks, about which there is little information, occurred in the vicinity of Pigeon Point. In 1851 the brig *Mary Stuart* ran aground at Point Año Nuevo. Sixty years later, the *Triton,* a German power schooner, collided with a drifting log and sank near Pigeon Point.

Six miles north of Pigeon Point is a perilous rock formation called Pescadero Point. Described by Coast Guard officials as "a nasty spot for vessels," Pescadero Point's foggy cliffs are treacherous. Several ships, unable to see the light or hear the signal at Pigeon Point, wrecked in the area including the fishing trawler *Iolanda* in 1923, the tanker *Tamiahua* in 1930, the purse seiner *New Crivello* in 1936, the freighter *West Mahwah* in 1937, and the fishing boat *Southland* in 1944.

Mary Stuart — June 20, 1851

Bound for Mazatlan, Mexico with sixty passengers and a cargo of quicksilver from San Francisco, the *Mary Stuart* foundered at Point Año Nuevo. Working all night in heavy seas, Capt. Charles Thompson and eight crew anchored a line ashore to rescue the stunned voyagers. They also salvaged most of the precious payload. Sadly, the pounding waves proved too powerful for the battered brig. She crumpled and sank into the breakers.

The ship had first sailed from New York to San Francisco in 1849 steering for the California goldfields. Soon after, she went into service between San Francisco and Panama.

Triton — **April 18, 1911**

The *Triton,* a German power schooner, struck a wandering log and sank thirteen miles off Pigeon Point. Two officers and nine crew saved themselves by rowing a lifeboat through rough seas to the lighthouse.

When she wrecked, the vessel was voyaging back to home port in the Marshall Islands. German trading firms had operated in the Marshalls since the 1860s. Annexed to Germany in 1885, the islands were a protectorate until they were captured by Japan in 1914.

Iolanda — **October 14, 1923**

Headed for fishing grounds off Santa Cruz, the *Iolanda* stranded at Pescadero Point on October 14, 1923. The fifty-three-ton fishing trawler went to pieces on the rocks.

Blinded by dense fog, Capt. W.H. Anderson and eight crew plunged overboard and swam for shore. Engineer Michael Bird was caught below deck tending the ship's machinery. His body washed ashore several hours after the others dragged themselves to safety.

Owned by San Francisco "Fish King" Achille Paladini, the largest wholesale seafood distributor on the West Coast, the vessel had been sailing for eighteen years.

Local news accounts indicated that within twenty minutes of striking the rocks, pieces of the vessel were scattered along the beach. "The *Iolanda* is a complete wreck," one report said, "not a board remaining intact."

Tamiahua — **November 6, 1930**

Sailing in heavy fog on November 6, 1930, the Richfield oil tanker *Tamiahua* ran aground near Pescadero Point. With a length of 500 feet, breadth of 71 feet, and measuring 10,000 tons, the vessel was said to be the largest tanker built on the Pacific Coast up to that time.

The tanker Tamiahua *on San Francisco Bay sometime after her launching.* Publisher's Collection.

Having discharged a cargo of oil in San Francisco, the *Tamiahua* steered for San Pedro. Capt. Gustave Andersen lost his bearings in fog so thick it obliterated the coastline. "While steaming south the ship became completely turned around," he admitted, "and beached while proceeding north."

A jagged reef punched a hole in the tanker's steel hull. Waves as high as eight feet flooded the engine room and swept over the stern. The hull began to buckle. As seas grew rougher, the *Tamiahua* flopped about like a giant beached whale.

Coast Guard cutters and four tugs arrived to help the stranded ship. Capt. Andersen and five of his forty-five crew members made perilous trips in a small boat, hauling steel towing lines from the tanker to the tugs. After four hours, the lines were strung. Unfortunately, the cables snapped and sank to the bottom of the sea.

More than 1,000 onlookers arrived in their automobiles from nearby towns. According to one report, "Hundreds stretched out on the beach, munching picnic lunches, and peering at the stricken tanker as it teetered and pivoted in the grip of the reef a scant 100 yards offshore."

Pumps and air compressors designed to lift the vessel were placed aboard, water was pumped out of the hold, and divers patched the hull. Tons of cement were placed under the hull to serve as a bridge over which the ship could slide from the reef. Curiosity seekers, awaiting the "Big Pull," continued their vigil.

Finally, with two power winches on the tanker's deck and steel cables rigged to huge kedge anchors dropped into the sea some distance from the stranded ship, the "Big Pull" began. Tugs stood by as the tanker strained to gain its freedom. The *Tamiahua* floated free, and was taken in tow to San Francisco.

Built at Oakland by Moore Shipyards in 1921, the hefty tanker was valued at $2 million. She had been stranded for nineteen days.

New Crivello — September 24, 1936

Carrying fifty tons of sardines, the *New Crivello* went ashore near Point Pinos Lighthouse in Monterey on September 18, 1936. The purse seiner, owned by Joe G. Crivello, was launched only a few weeks before the mishap.

Thousands of dead sardines lined the beach after the wreck. "The sea gulls were quick to discover this free feed," one newspaper commented, "and came in brigades to take advantage of it."

Capt. Mike Lucido blamed heavy fog for the accident. Luckily, he and ten crew made their way to shore in a skiff. Refloated three days later by the tug *Sea Salvor*, the new seiner seemed saved, as well.

Partially submerged, the 116-ton vessel was towed toward San Francisco for repairs. Unfortunately, the *Sea Salvor's* slings snapped while passing Pigeon Point Lighthouse. On September 24, 1936, the *New Crivello* sank two miles off Pescadero Point.

West Mahwah — July 9, 1937

The freighter *West Mahwah* stranded on a sand-spit 300 yards off Pescadero Point on July 9, 1937. The ship crashed ashore in thick "pea-soup" fog.

One of the largest vessels owned by the McCormick Steamship Company, the *West Mahwah* measured 8,800 tons. Recently sailing from Puget Sound, the ship carried a deck load of lumber and general cargo bound for New York. Aboard were forty-five crew and two passengers, one of them a young woman.

Listing sharply to starboard, the *West Mahwah's* cargo shifted, breaking the boilers from their foundations and settling the ship on the bottom. Passenger Karola Preer sprained her ankle on the sloping deck. Nevertheless, Capt. E.A. Jensen radioed, "No immediate or great danger. Everything quiet."

Coast Guard vessels rushed to the scene, but dense fog hampered rescue efforts. Tugs tried vainly to free the freighter from the sand. During one attempt to pull the *West Mahwah* free, a snapping line whipped across the deck striking seaman Edward Goodwin. Suffering a fractured arm and broken nose, he was carried off the ship and sent to a hospital in San Francisco.

The ship's "pea-soup" dilemma proved a problem for local ranchers as well. Complaining that his pea crop was being trodden into the

The house flag of the McCormick Steamship Co. included a red letter M inside a blue star on a white background. Publisher's Collection.

ground, one coastal farmer ordered rescue crews off his land. When curiosity seekers began crossing his property, the farmer resorted to charging admission. "The receipts," he claimed, "fell far short of the damage to the pea crop."

On July 11th, after jettisoning a quarter of her lumber, the *West Mahwah* was dragged from the sand and towed to San Francisco for repairs. Valued at $10,000, the abandoned lumber lay on ranch land adjoining the beach. Longingly, local residents hovered over the immense stack. "Pescadero people would have enough cut lumber to erect barns and homes for the next fifty years," one observer said. The pea farmer may have made a profit after all.

Southland — September 26, 1944

The *Southland*, a 62-ton fishing boat built in 1930, went ashore on September 26, 1944. Perched on the beach below Pescadero Point for three weeks, the vessel was salvaged by her owners at high tide.

About the Author

Appendix

Sources

Index

About the Author

JoAnn Semones, Ph.D., boarded her first ship at age three. The voyage, made aboard the military transport vessel *E.D. Patrick*, left a lasting impression. She has loved sea sagas ever since.

Born on an Army Air Force base in Midland, Texas, JoAnn traveled from post to post with her parents and younger sister, eventually settling in California. After graduating from California State University, Northridge, with a degree in journalism, she worked as a small town newspaper reporter and photographer.

JoAnn also enjoyed a brief stint on Capitol Hill as press secretary to a California Congressman, and later held management positions with the U.S. Small Business Administration and the U.S. Environmental Protection Agency. Over the course of her career, JoAnn has written many newspaper and magazine articles and given numerous speeches, workshops, seminars, and media interviews. Along the way, she earned M.A. and Ph.D. degrees in public policy.

As a consultant with the Monterey Bay National Marine Sanctuary, JoAnn developed concepts and text for the new Pigeon Point Lighthouse Interpretive Center. Currently, she is writing a book for the exhibit and conducting research for another volume on shipwrecks.

JoAnn's stories have appeared in a variety of publications, including *Mains'L Haul, Professional Mariner, Anchor Light, A Light In The Mist*, and *Surviving Magazine*, as well as in Stanford University's anthology, *Learning to Live Again*, and in the *Chicken Soup for the Soul* international book series.

She lives in the picturesque coastal town of Half Moon Bay, California.

APPENDIX

THOSE WHO WERE LOST

Sir John Franklin — **January 17, 1865**

Edward J. Church — seaman
Capt. John Despeau — ship's master
John Devine — seaman
Charles Martin — seaman
Robert Dawson Owens — supercargo
John Sooltine — seaman
Jacob Staten — seaman
Unidentified — five crew

Coya — **November 24, 1866**

Frank Bashby — carpenter
William Carr — second mate
John Cooper — seaman
Buquemy English — seaman
"James" — cook
Mr. & Mrs. Jeffreys & child — passengers from Portsmouth
Peter Johnson — seaman (lost during the voyage)
John Jones — seaman
Mrs. Laisetta — passenger from Napa Valley
James Martin — stowaway
P. McNamara — seaman
Frederick Myers — seaman

George Owens — seaman
Capt. & Mrs. H. Paige & daughter — ship's master & family
Mrs. Pearson — passenger from San Francisco
Dr. & Mrs. Rowden — passengers from London
Peter Shannon — ship's boy
James Skelton — sailmaker
James Smith — seaman
John Smith — steward
Tom Smith — seaman
Oliver Tom — seaman

Hellespont — November 18, 1868

John Baptiste — seaman
William Brimer — seaman
James King — seaman
Olorf Peterson — seaman
John Smith — seaman
Capt. Cornelius Soule — ship's master
Charles Williams — seaman
"Wilson" — first mate
Unidentified — three crew

J.W. Seaver — April 10, 1887

John Moore — second mate
Eduard Samuelson — seaman
Unidentified — cook

San Vicente — December 20, 1887

Alfred Clark — seaman
Marvin Clinton — fireman
Louis Everett — purser
John Grady — seaman
Charles Graham — seaman
Thomas Grimes — assistant engineer
R. Jackson — steward

John McArdle — chief engineer
"Sam" — steward
Fred Smith — seaman
Jack Wilcox — seaman
Unidentified — fireman

Iolanda — October 14, 1923

Michael Bird — engineer

San Juan — August 29, 1929

Capt. Adolf F. Asplund — age 65, master of *San Juan*
Willis Barton — age 19, café worker
H. Beardsley — age unknown, *San Juan* cabin watchman
Vera Kliffmiller Bell — age 27, housewife
D. Bohan — age unknown, *San Juan* fireman
Willie Jasmine Brown — age 29, housewife
Lewis Gordon Burris — age 65, steam engineer
Jose Cazares — age 21, property manager
Jack B. Cleveland — age 47, *San Juan* purser
Harry Colvin — age 28, baggage porter
George Constantine Constandarus — age unknown, *San Juan*
        seaman
T. Curran — age unknown, *San Juan* engineer
John Doherty — age 68, *San Juan* fireman
E. Dovershall — age and occupation unknown
J. Durrand — age unknown, *San Juan* cook
James O. Edler — age 77, retired
Ida H. Eley — age 42, beauty parlor owner
Fred England — age and occupation unknown
Albert Estrada — age unknown, *San Juan* waiter
C.F. Fersen — age and occupation unknown
Harriett Louise Field — age 73, housewife
S. Fisher — age and occupation unknown
Josephine Foley — age unknown, housewife
Mrs. E. Fraser — age unknown, housewife
William Fuchs — age 37, importer
A. Gonzales — age unknown, *San Juan* mess boy
Emma Grandstedt — age 48, housewife

Anna Marie Hansen — age 32, secretary
Erik Morten Hansen — age 4, child
Ole Hansen — age 7, child
William J. Hawthorne — age 45, bank employee
Mr. & Mrs. Hill — age and occupation unknown
Arthur Frederick Hillbranch — age 29, hardware store
     employee
Gladys Elizabeth Hincks (aka Betty Simmons) — age 20,
     housewife
Lilla Kendall — age unknown, housewife
Ernest Knight — age unknown, *San Juan* waiter
Ernest Lang — age unknown, *San Juan* cook
G. Lavelle — age and occupation unknown
A.P. MacNeil — age and occupation unknown
E.D. Marshall — age and occupation unknown
Elizabeth Mason — age 31, housewife
Martha Mason — age 7, child
M. Mathews — age and occupation unknown
R.R. Minner — age and occupation unknown
C. Mitchell — age unknown, *San Juan* waiter
Ingebor Louise Mohler — age 54, "newlywed"
Julius Moore — age and occupation unknown
Frank F. Moses — age 25, occupation unknown
Mrs. F. M. Moses — age unknown, housewife
George Navarro — age 17, movie extra
James Norton — age unknown, *San Juan* chief engineer
Anna Olson — age 60, housewife
Helen Olson — age 29, retail store employee
John Olson — age 64, retail store owner
Jesus Rulfo Perez — age 32, tax collector of wines and liquors
Mr. & Mrs. L.W. Petersen — age and occupation unknown
Marjorie Pifer — age 27, housewife
Juan Perez Sanchez — age 38, land owner
R. Schellens — age and occupation unknown
Leslie L. Seabury — age 28, Union Oil Company employee
Sara Seitz — age unknown, businesswoman
Clara Slater Shepard — age 66, housewife
Mary Everson Slater — age unknown, "maiden lady"
A. Torres — age unknown, *San Juan* mess boy
James W. Turner — age unknown, *San Juan* waiter

L. Valentine — age and occupation unknown
Antone Verducci — age 41, *San Juan* steward
A. Von Bunk — age unknown, *San Juan* seaman
Paul Wagner — age 23, teacher
George Watts — age 51, *San Juan* cook
Charles M. Welsted — age 40, businessman
Max Wilkes — age 29, nurse
Unidentified — a *San Juan* engineer

BARC 1 — **March 17, 1953**

Marshall W. Esslinger — captain
Mario Fontanella — crewman
William R. Grajciar — crew chief

BIBLIOGRAPHY

General

Brinnin, John Malcolm. *The Sway of the Grand Saloon.* New York, New York: Delacorte Press, 1971.

Clark, Arthur Hamilton. *The Clipper Ship Era 1843-1869.* Riverside, Connecticut: 7 C's Press, 1970.

Gibbs, James. *Shipwrecks of the Pacific Coast.* Portland, Oregon: Binford and Mort, 1962.

La Grange, Jacques and Helen. *Clipper Ships of America and Great Britain 1833-1869.* New York, New York: G.P. Putnam's Sons, 1936.

Kemble, John Haskell. *The Panama Route.* Berkeley, California: University of California Press, 1943.

Marshall, Don. *California Shipwrecks.* Seattle, Washington: Superior Publishing Company, 1978.

Morrall, June. *Half Moon Bay Memories.* El Granada, California: Moonbeam Press, 1987.

Perry, Frank. *The History of Pigeon Point Lighthouse.* Santa Cruz, California: Otter B Books, 1995.

Reinstedt, Randall. *Shipwrecks and Sea Monsters.* Carmel, California: Ghost Town Publications, 1975.

Record of Wreck Reports, U.S. Coast Guard, National Archives and Records Administration

Rogers, John G. *Origins Of Sea Terms.* Mystic, Connecticut: Mystic Seaport Museum, 1985.

Shipwreck Data Base, National Marine Sanctuary Program, National Oceanic and Atmospheric Administration

Volo, Dorothy D. and James M. *Daily Life In The Age Of Sail.* Westport, Connecticut: Greenwood Press, 2002.

Carrier Pigeon

"Carrier Pigeon," *Prices Current and Shipping List*, 15 June 1853.

"Carrier Pigeon," *Weekly Mirror*, Bath, Maine, 1 January 1853.

"Loss of the Carrier Pigeon," *New York Daily Tribune*, 12 July 1853.

"Loss of the Clipper Ship *Carrier Pigeon*," *San Francisco Herald*, 8 June 1853.

"Loss of Clipper Ship *Carrier Pigeon*," *Weekly Mirror*, Bath, Maine, 16 July 1853.

"Naming of Pigeon Point," *San Mateo County Times-Gazette*, 21 February 1903.

"Steamer Sea Bird Ashore," *Daily Alta California*, 13 June 1853.

"Wreck of the *Carrier Pigeon*," *Daily Alta California*, 8 June 1853.

"Wreck of the *Carrier Pigeon*," *Daily Alta California*, 10 June 1853.

Sir John Franklin

"Aboard A Transatlantic Packet," *Ocean Navigator*, September/October 2002.

"San Mateo's Graveyard of Sailing Ships," *San Mateo County Times*, 30 September 1972.

"Shipwreck," *San Mateo County Gazette*, 21 January 1865.

"Shipwreck and Loss of Life," *San Francisco Bulletin*, 19 January 1865.

"*Sir John Franklin* Lost," *Daily Alta California*, 19 January 1865.

"Wreck of the *Sir John Franklin*," *Daily Alta California*, 24 January 1865.

"Wreck of the *Sir John Franklin*," *San Mateo County Gazette*, 11 February 1865.

"Wrecked Ship *Sir John Franklin*," *San Francisco Evening Bulletin*, 23 January 1865.

Coya & Hellespont

Coroner investigation and jury report on the shipwreck *Coya*, 1866.

Frederick Wilson, statement to San Francisco Board of Inquiry on shipwreck *Hellespont*, 1868.

"From The Wreck," *San Mateo County Gazette*, 31 November 1866.

"*Hellespont* Wrecked At Pescadero," *San Mateo County Gazette*, 21 November 1868.

"Lighthouse Needed," *San Mateo County Gazette*, 28 November 1868.

"Loss of the *Hellespont*," *San Mateo County Gazette*, 28 November 1868.

"Loss of the Ship *Hellespont*," *New York Times*, 9 December 1868.

"Tales of Shipwrecks," *Pacifica Tribune*, 5 April 1989.

"Wreck of the British Bark *Coya*," *San Mateo County Gazette*, 1 December 1866.

"Wreck of the Ship *Hellespont*," *San Francisco Bulletin*, 20 November 1868.

J.W. Seaver & San Vicente

"Bark Wrecked," *The Daily Surf*, 12 April 1887.

Best, Gerald M. *The Story of the Pacific Coast Company.* Berkeley, California: Howell-North, 1964.

Nelson, Sharlene and Ted. *Umbrella Guide to California Lighthouses.* Portland, Oregon: Epicenter Press, 1993.

Piwarzyk, Robert W., "Laguna Limekilns," manuscript, 1996.

"Sea Disasters Befall Steamers Long Ago," *Half Moon Bay Review*, 27 November 1969.

"Steamer *San Vicente* Burns," *Nautical Brass*, May/June 1991.

"Tales of Shipwrecks," *Pacifica Tribune*, 16 August 1989.

Colombia

"Awash To Her 'Tween Decks," reprint of news article. 17 July 1896.

"*Columbia* Cannot Be Saved," *San Francisco Examiner*, 16 July 1896.

"Eleven Thousand Miles East and West," Pacific Mail Steamship Company handbook, 1896.

Lastreto, Carlos. "I Was On The Wrecked *Colombia*," *Peninsula Life*, April 1948.

"Loss Of The *Colombia*," *San Mateo County Times Gazette*, 18 July 1896.

"No Hope For The Stranded Steamer," *San Francisco Chronicle*, 16 July 1896.

"On The Rocks In A Dense Fog," *San Francisco Examiner*, 15 July 1896.

"Residents Profit By The Wreck Of The *Colombia*," *San Francisco Chronicle*, 7 May 1897.

"Steamer *Colombia* Wrecked In A Fog," *San Francisco Chronicle*, 15 July 1896.

"Wreckers At Work On The *Colombia*," *San Francisco Chronicle*, 18 July 1896.

Point Arena

"Chutes And Cables," *Alta Vista Magazine*, 8 August 1993.

"Coastal History," *Cen Cal News*, Vol. X, No. 6., date unknown.

Conant, Edward. *Memories of Gazos Creek and Pigeon Point: 1916-1918*. Modesto, California: Glenhaven Press, 1998.

Cox, Thomas R. *Mills and Markets: A History of the Pacific Lumber Industry to 1900*. Seattle, Washington: University of Washington Press, 1974.

Evans, Colonel Albert S. "A La California," book excerpt, 1873.

"Steamer Wrecked At Pigeon Point," *San Francisco Chronicle*, 10 August 1913.

"Tales of Shipwrecks," *Pacifica Tribune*, 1989.

Pilgrim

Allen, Everett S. *The Black Ships: Rumrunners of Prohibition*. Boston: Little, Brown and Company, 1979.

Canney, Donald L. "Rum War: The U.S. Coast Guard And Prohibition," manuscript, January 1998.

"Dry Agents Rush To Liquor Hunt," *Half Moon Bay Review*, 6 June 1925.

"Heavily Laden Liquor Ship Is Captured," *Half Moon Bay Review*, 20 June 1925.

Mygrants, Jessie. Interview at Pigeon Point Lighthouse, 26 April 1987.

"Rum Boat Cited Off County Coast," *Half Moon Bay Review*, 27 June 1925.

"Rum Runner On Rocks Today At Pigeon Point," *San Mateo Times*, 22 May 1925.

"Rum Ship On Rocks At Pigeon Point," *Redwood City Tribune*, 22 May 1925.

"Rum Ships Go On Rocks," *Half Moon Bay Review*, 23 May 1925.

Severn, Bill. *The End of the Roaring Twenties*. New York: Julian Messner, 1969.

"Two Beached Liquor Boats Are Caught," *San Francisco Chronicle*, 23 May 1925.

Willoughby, Malcolm. *Rum War At Sea*. Washington, D.C.: U.S. Government Printing Office, 1964.

San Juan

"Blunders Held Cause of Fatal Crash," *Burlingame Advance Star*, 30 August 1929.

"Captain Last Sighted Clinging To Bridge," *San Francisco Chronicle*, 31 August 1929.

"Cowardice Seen In Ship Tragedy," *San Mateo Times*, 31 August 1929.

"Officers Face Inquiry," *San Francisco Chronicle*, 1 September 1929.

San Juan Trial Decision, 16 October 1929.

Spinelli, Lorraine. Interview with the author, 3 July 2001.

Statements to inspectors, 31 August 1929 to 11 September 1929.

"Survivors Reach S.F.," *San Mateo Times*, 30 August 1929.

Testimony taken at appeal of Robert Papenfuss, 22 November 1929.

"Three Face Trial In *San Juan* Wreck," *San Francisco Chronicle*, 6 September 1929.

Western Spirit & Ohio No. 3

"Boat Aground, Crew Is Saved," *San Mateo Times*, 18 September 1934.

"Eleven Saved In Wreck Of Fishing Craft," *San Francisco Chronicle*, 3 February 1932.

Kemp, Michael Kenneth. *Cannery Row: The History Of Old Ocean View Avenue.* Pacific Grove, California: The History Company, 1986.

"*Ohio No.3* Safe In S.F. Shipyard," *Monterey Peninsula Herald*, 21 September 1934.

Petrich, Allen. Interview with the author, 19 April 2006.

"Purse Seiner Wrecked," *Monterey Peninsula Herald*, 2 February 1932.

"Seiner Piles Up At Pigeon Point," *San Francisco Chronicle*, 18 September 1934.

"Snow Squalls Drive Trawler On Rocks," *San Mateo Times*, 2 February 1932.

"Wrecked Purser May Be Salvaged," *Monterey Peninsula Herald*, 19 September 1934.

"Wrecked Purser Towed," *Monterey Peninsula Herald*, 20 September 1934.

BARC 1

Amphibious Lighter Operators Handbook, U.S. Army Technical Manual, January 1965.

"Army Amphib Salvaging Ships," *Monterey Peninsula Herald*, 24 February 1953.

"Army Board Reports On BARC Sinking," *Monterey Peninsula Herald*, 11 June 1953.

"BARC Invades Monterey," *Monterey Peninsula Herald*, 13 February 1953.

"$100,000 Bite Will Get You A BARC," *St. Petersburg Times*, 5 December 2003.

"Both Skippers Blamed For BARC Disaster," *Monterey Peninsula Herald*, 22 April 1953.

"Land And Sea Craft Sinks Off Coast," *San Mateo Times*, 18 March 1953.

"New Type of Amphib Lost With Three Aboard," *San Francisco Chronicle*, 18 March 1953.

Poulter, Thomas Charles. *Over The Years*. College Park, Maryland: American Institute of Physics, 1978.

"Presenting The BARC," research project briefing paper, Army Transportation Corps, 1952.

"Purse Seiner Sinks Under Tow To S.F.," *Monterey Peninsula Herald*, 26 February 1953.

Research For Industry, SRI International, Vol. V, No. 3, March 1953.

"Three Crewmen Lost As Giant BARC Sinks," *Monterey Peninsula Herald*, 18 March 1953.

Mary Stuart

"Ashore," *Daily Alta California*, 21 June 1851.

Triton

Merchants Exchange Annual Report, 1910-1911.

Iolanda

"*Iolanda* Survivors In S.F. Hospital," *Monterey Peninsula Herald*, 17 October 1923.

"Trawler Hits Rocks, One Dead," *Half Moon Bay Review*, 20 October 1923.

"Vessel Driven On Rocks," *Santa Cruz Evening News*, 15 October 1923.

Tamiahua

"Crew Clings To Tanker," *San Francisco Chronicle*, 10 November 1930.

"Hawser Snaps As Tugs Aid Vessel," *San Francisco Chronicle*, 8 November 1930.

"New Hope For Beached Tanker," *San Mateo Times*, 10 November 1930.

"Sailors Stand By Captain," *San Francisco Chronicle*, 9 November 1930.

"Stranded Tanker Floated," *San Mateo Times*, 25 November 1930.

"Tanker Breaking Up On Pescadero Reef," *San Mateo Times*, 8 November 1930.

"Tanker Pounds To Pieces," *San Francisco Chronicle*, 7 November 1930.

"Tugs Fail To Float Big Tanker," *San Mateo Times*, 7 November 1930.

New Crivello

"*New Crivello* Towed To S.F.," *Monterey Peninsula Herald*, 22 September, 1936.

"Purse Seiner Total Loss," *Monterey Peninsula Herald*, 25 September 1936.

"Seiner Drifts Ashore On Reefs," *Monterey Peninsula Herald*, 19 September 1936.

West Mahwah

"Big S.F. Freighter On Rocks," *San Francisco Chronicle*, 9 July 1937.

"Big S.F. Freighter Still Helpless," *San Francisco Chronicle*, 10 July 1937.

"Cutter, Tug Refloat Big S.F. Vessel," *San Francisco Chronicle*, 11 July, 1937.

"47 In Peril On Wrecked Ship," *San Mateo Times*, 9 July 1937

"Stricken Ship Returns To S.F.," *San Francisco Chronicle*, 12 July 1937.

"Wrecked Ship Moves To S.F.," *San Mateo Times*, 12 July 1937.

"Wrecked Ship Unloads Cargo," *San Mateo Times*, 10 July 1937.

Southland

"Pescadero News," *Half Moon Bay Review*, 12 October 1944.

INDEX